Series/Number 07-113

CW01081931

COMPUTATIONAL MODELING

CHARLES S. TABER
RICHARD J. TIMPONE
State University of New York at Stony Brook

SAGE PUBLICATIONS
International Educational and Professional Publisher
Thousand Oaks   London   New Delhi

For information address:

SAGE Publications, Inc.
2455 Teller Road
Thousand Oaks, California 91320
E-mail: order@sagepub.com

SAGE Publications Ltd.
6 Bonhill Street
London EC2A 4PU
United Kingdom

SAGE Publications India Pvt. Ltd.
M-32 Market
Greater Kailash I
New Delhi, 110 048 India

Printed in the United States of America

Library of Congress Cataloging-in-Publication Data

Taber, Charles S.
    Computational modeling / authors, Charles S. Taber and Richard J. Timpone.
       p. cm. — (Sage university papers series. Quantitative applications
in the social sciences; no. 07-113)
    Includes bibliographical references.
    ISBN 0-8039-7270-9 (pbk.: acid-free paper)
    1. Social sciences—Mathematical models. 2. Social sciences—Data
processing. I. Timpone, Richard J. II. Title. III. Series.
H61.T23 1996
003'.3—dc20   95-50246

96 97 98 99 10 9 8 7 6 5 4 3 2 1

Sage Production Editor: Gillian Dickens

When citing a university paper, please use the proper form. Remember to cite the current Sage University Paper series title and include the proper number. One of the following formats can be adapted (depending on the style manual used).

(1) TABER, CHARLES S., and TIMPONE, R. J. (1996) *Computational Modeling*. Sage University Paper series on Quantitative Applications in the Social Sciences, 07-113. Thousand Oaks, CA: Sage.

OR

(2) Taber, C. S., & Timpone, R. J. (1996) *Computational Modeling* (Sage University Paper series on Quantitative Applications in the Social Sciences, series no. 07-113). Thousand Oaks, CA: Sage.

CONTENTS

ACKNOWLEDGMENTS

A number of our colleagues contributed directly or indirectly to this monograph. Joel Kaji, Kenneth Rona, Jeffrey Segal, and Michael Young each read a working paper that became the core of Chapters 1 and 5. We are very grateful for their comments and suggestions, which ultimately convinced us to try a longer work. Stanley Feldman and Mark Schneider each answered questions that had us puzzled while we were writing the first draft. The series reviewers provided detailed suggestions and highly constructive criticism on the first draft, which led to several structural improvements. We owe a huge debt to the many friends and colleagues who helped us with earlier work. Although they remain anonymous here, they are acknowledged in our earlier computational modeling papers on foreign policy decision making (POLI), candidate evaluation (CANDI), social choice (the "dot program"), and foreign policy event interpretation (EVIN). We are particularly grateful to Philip Schrodt. Most of our published work on computational modeling, including this monograph, has benefited tremendously from the quality and quantity of his comments. The National Science Foundation supported our research directly under grants SES-9102901 and SES-9310351, and indirectly under grant DIR-9113599 to the Mershon Center Research Training Group on the Role of Cognition in Collective Political Decision Making at The Ohio State University. Finally, we owe special thanks to our families for their continuing support: Sue, Kathleen, and Christopher.

SERIES EDITOR'S INTRODUCTION

Progress in the social sciences can be measured by the acquisition of more and better tools. Since the 1960s, perhaps the most important new tool has been the computer. In the Quantitative Applications in the Social Sciences monograph series, we have titles directly relevant to computer users: *Microcomputer Methods for Social Scientists, 2nd Edition* (No. 40, Schrodt), *Using Microcomputers in Research* (No. 52, Madron, Tate, & Brookshire), and *Computer-Assisted Interviewing* (No. 80, Saris). More broadly, the quantitative procedures featured in all the monographs almost always require a computer. Computers are able to do more than provide data storage and statistical manipulations. As Professors Taber and Timpone observe, computers themselves have an analytic role in what the authors call computational modeling.

Professors Taber and Timpone organize disparate methods of computational modeling into three global types of models: dynamic simulation, knowledge-based systems, and machine learning. Behind each type is a social theory, to be written as a computer program. The first approach, dynamic simulation, is the oldest and most popular. A set of equations representing part of the world, for example, arms races, has its values systematically altered by the computer. The subsequent changes in outcomes then are observed. To the extent that the model reflects reality, the alterations inform us about what might actually happen under different conditions. To illustrate dynamic simulation, the authors work through a problem in bureaucratic politics and budget setting. They go on to explain cellular automata (a subset of dynamic simulations involving spatial representations).

The second type, knowledge-based systems, is part of the artificial intelligence (AI) tradition. Taber and Timpone examine semantic networks, frame systems, hybrid systems, and expert systems. (On the last, see also in this series *Expert Systems*, No. 77, by Benfer, Brent, & Furbee.) What holds these systems together is that they store information by computer in an effort to represent human knowledge. Semantic networks treat knowledge as a web of concept nodes and links. As an example, the authors explore how interviewees in a survey formulate their responses to political questions. Most frequently, AI work is based on expert systems. Knowledge about some specific area, say statistics or mountain climbing, is organized as a collection of "if-then" rules. The rules then are drawn on to help make decisions.

Machine-learning models differ from AI in that they are not committed to representing human knowledge. A common approach here is ID3, which aims to derive classification rules from the data themselves. The authors give the example of trying to account for different enrollment levels among ten high schools.

Computational modeling is a research method, one to be learned like any other. One of its advantages is that it forces theoretical precision. At the same time, it allows incorporation of numerous variables and values. In a certain sense, it permits a unique blend of the qualitative and the quantitative. Computational modeling will increase as computers become even more accessible and powerful. This monograph provides a good introduction to the many pathways that can be taken in this growing field.

—*Michael S. Lewis-Beck*
Series Editor

COMPUTATIONAL MODELING

CHARLES S. TABER
RICHARD J. TIMPONE
State University of New York at Stony Brook

1. INTRODUCTION

Beyond Platforms and On-Ramps

Computers have opened a new world in the few decades since their creation. Across all of society, as well as in academia, computers have revolutionized our lives. Social scientists use them primarily in two ways: as platforms for programs that facilitate general tasks such as word processing and statistical analysis and, increasingly, as on-ramps for the information superhighway, which has greatly increased the speed and volume of scholarly discourse. These two areas do not exhaust the utility of computers in the social sciences: Computers offer more than platforms and on-ramps. They can serve as special-purpose analytic tools.

The social sciences have seen a rising trend in the use of computational modeling over the last three decades. For several reasons, we believe that this trend will accelerate. First, computers are far more powerful, reliable, and affordable than ever before. Contemporary personal computers based on Pentium or RISC processors have similar capabilities to the supercomputers of a few years ago. Second, because of advances in operating systems, software packages, and programming tools, computers are now much easier to use. First-generation computational modelers programmed directly in machine language, which in some cases meant that they had to physically plug and unplug circuits. Although technical skill still helps in computational modeling, programming is now far less arcane, and special software packages bring computational modeling even closer to nonprogrammers. Third, there also have been many important advances in computational modeling methods, the topic of this monograph. Special-purpose methods, often woven from a particular theoretical framework, have been developed for classes of modeling problems. For example, decision making can be modeled using information-processing methods

1

developed in cognitive and organizational science, and adaptation can be modeled using genetic algorithms from math and computer science. In short, computational modeling will grow in importance for social scientists because computers and computer methods are far more powerful and accessible than ever before. The increase in computational modeling that we anticipate will depend most directly on how much practical utility social scientists see in these methods for the problems that interest them. In this monograph, we treat computational models as a single broad class of methods and discuss their merits in general terms. By contrast, social scientists (as opposed to computer scientists or engineers) generally treat computer-based methods piecemeal, not seeing them as part of a single framework. The piecemeal approach, unfortunately, diffuses recognition of the general utility of computational models and deflects consideration of their potential contribution to the growth of theoretical knowledge. It is instructive to note that the domain of statistical analysis similarly subsumes a wide variety of different tools, all of which spring from a single broad set of unifying assumptions, and that the utility of statistics for social scientists was recognized only after the epistemological framework of the behavioral revolution had taken firm hold (and after computers and software made the tools generally available). We therefore take a broader view of computational modeling than those who would apply the label only to a single method, such as dynamic simulation or artificial intelligence. In the following chapters, we will tour a wide variety of different approaches, divided into three general categories: dynamic simulation (e.g., Monte Carlo methods), knowledge-based models (semantic networks, frame systems, and rule-based systems), and machine-learning models (connectionism, ID3, and genetic algorithms). In this chapter and in the remainder of the monograph, we will focus on their similarities.

Models and Computational Models

At the risk of offending some philosophical purists (see, e.g., Brodbeck, 1969), we will use the terms "model" and "theory" rather loosely, defining a model to be a representation of a theory about some real-world phenomenon. Models are integral in the development of theoretical understanding. They fill the gap in the essential interplay between theory and data, allowing empirical regularities to guide theory (induction) and allowing theory to guide empirical analysis (deduction).

To express theories—that is, to build models—we have three general languages to choose from (Ostrom, 1988). These are natural language, various dialects of mathematics (including statistics and logic), and computational symbolic processing. Although one may reasonably argue that all complete formal languages are intertranslatable, making computational symbolic processing and classical mathematics formally interchangeable (Turing, 1950), that would obscure an important practical distinction: Computational symbolic processing allows us to do many things that are only theoretically possible without the aid of a computer. Conversely, some things are done more easily mathematically, including theorem proving and anything dealing with infinities. Worse, such an argument would bog us down in painful philosophical debate, and our basic point would remain intact: Symbolic manipulation on a computer, like math or English, provides a general language for expressing scientific theories about the world.

Computational models, then, are theories rendered as computer programs. For example, McPhee (1963) developed a model of social influence on voting behavior that represents theoretical processes such as "discussion" and "learning" as symbolic relationships in a computer program. The implications of the entire theoretical structure then can be drawn by literally "running the model" and observing how it behaves. More generally, computational modeling entails developing a process theory, expressing this theory as a computer program, and simulating the theory by running the program. The seemingly distinct tools described in Chapters 2 through 4 generally follow this basic pattern of analysis. Moreover, when expressing and simulating theoretical models through the medium of computer programs, similar concerns of validation arise (Chapter 5).

Why Model Computationally?

There are many forms of analysis in the social sciences, including qualitative case studies, quantitative data analyses, and mathematical models. In our view, scientific knowledge can accumulate through careful research along any of these paths (cf. King, Keohane, & Verba, 1994). No single approach can suffice for all research problems in the social sciences. Indeed, many problems require multimethod research. Computational modeling is another approach that can be added to this list. Why do so?

A variety of advantages of formal over natural-language models have been documented (Fiorina, 1975), all of which pertain to both mathematical and computational work: (a) the definitional and conceptual precision of the model, (b) the clarity of assumptions, (c) the ease of deciding on its internal or logical validity, (d) the power of formal deduction, and (e) the relatively unambiguous communication among scientists using formal language. For Fiorina (1975, p. 138), "the major advantage of using formal models is the precision and clarity of thought which these models require, and the depth of argument which they allow." He quickly acknowledges the main limitation of mathematical models: "Doubters would argue that intellectual clarity is purchased at too dear a price, that it involves simplifying reality beyond all recognition." In subsequent paragraphs, he unhappily endorses the goal of predictive accuracy as paramount in scientific explanation: "A modeler tends to brush off criticisms that his models are hopelessly unrealistic. With no real expectation of finding the one, true explanation, he settles for one which works, i.e., predicts more accurately than anything else available." This was a reasonable response, in our view. Predictive accuracy and analytic focus cannot be sacrificed. Fortunately, however, computational methods allow scientists to model rigorously the complex process mechanisms that they may theorize.

This is the major advantage of computational over mathematical modeling: It greatly increases the level of realism one may incorporate in a formal model without sacrificing analytic focus. In research areas in which formal models become intractable, the computational approach allows one to aspire to achieve both predictive and process validity. We want to be very clear, however, that when research problems that account for process are solvable within a mathematical model, computational modeling may be unnecessary.

Some readers may be skeptical, however, believing that we are confusing descriptive accuracy with theoretical explanation. Our main argument for computational modeling, after all, is that it allows us to increase the descriptive realism of our models. Nevertheless, computational models remain models and are simplifications. We see a qualitative difference between a simplified representation of a real-world process and a model that treats the process as a black box, making no attempt at representing the real-world process. The former is a caricature with recognizable features and may facilitate theoretical explanation; the latter is not even a caricature. Most of the computational methods described in this monograph are designed to represent theoretical processes, though they vary in the "depth" of process detail they can express. For those who seek process-valid explanations, computational modeling can help with the added theoretical complexity.

Because our argument hinges on the distinction between accurate prediction and the understanding of process, a digression on this point may be helpful. Prediction focuses on the output of a theoretical model, treated as a black box, that may be compared to factors in the real world; explanation, in contrast, focuses on the model itself, illuminating the formerly black box so that we can examine the process mechanisms that produce the output. Most sciences have gone through phases corresponding to the different goals of predictive success and explanation. Dissatisfaction with pure prediction usually arises when it becomes clear that basic assumptions are false or when several quite different models accurately predict the data. At this point, controversy usually erupts between those who are interested in learning more about the actual mechanisms involved and those fully satisfied with correct predictions. Astronomers in the late 16th century, for example, fought this battle. Most Copernicans were satisfied with the highly unlikely system of interlocking epicycles that they had fashioned to account for the irregular planetary orbits they observed. After all, the system worked, in that it was reasonably accurate in predicting planetary paths and compiling navigational charts. What did it matter that the mechanisms for this calculation were "geometrical fictions" (Koestler, 1959, p. 171)? Johannes Kepler, however, could not accept this view and devoted his life to uncovering the processes actually at work in planetary motion. He sought a deeper understanding, and in retrospect, the science of astronomy could not have advanced without adopting his ethic. Predictive success was necessary but was insufficient for explanation.

Past work, across the social sciences, has demonstrated the merits of computational modeling (Hastie, 1988; Taber & Timpone, 1994a). First, although computational models, like mathematical models, enforce precision and clarity of thought, they allow for theoretical uncertainty when necessary. It can be very difficult to deal with the inevitable holes in our theoretical understanding within a tractable mathematical model. In contrast, computational models are "cheap" and highly flexible. When faced with unknown pieces of the puzzle, a computational modeler can fill the holes temporarily with random variables, or, with relatively little additional cost in time or effort, one may simulate several hypothetical subprocesses to fill the holes and examine their competing implications.

Second, computational methods are more versatile than other formal approaches. Theoretical concepts that would be very difficult to express using standard mathematics (e.g., semantic networks in cognitive models) can be represented computationally. Moreover, most concepts or relations expressible in mathematics or logic also can be expressed computationally. The range of theoretical statements that can be made in a formal model therefore is dramatically increased.

Third, although computational models are designed to reflect reality, they are not constrained by it. As King, Keohane, and Verba (1994) state, "inferences are necessarily uncertain because the world was not designed to make life easy for social scientists: the opportunities to run true experiments are very rare." Computational models allow the explicit examination of counterfactual data and situations, even when the underlying theory is complex. Although these results remain driven by the assumptions of the model (which are explicit and therefore can be critiqued readily), they can test "what if" questions that may be of interest but are not necessarily manipulable (e.g., the impact of different levels of urbanization on traditional western African societies).

Fourth, the computational approach offers far more deductive power than the alternatives. As Hastie (1988, p. 426) points out in the context of social psychology, "theory development seems to occur in a progression from concrete empirical findings, to low-level generalizations, to increasingly general and integrative theoretical structures." The bottleneck in this progression is the theoretical step in which several disparate empirical findings are integrated into a coherent whole from which new predictions can be made and tested. Computational simulation is a powerful method for inferring the combined implications of several theoretical assumptions or empirical results.

The most important advantage of computational models, as a domain, is the ability to represent complex processes as well as predict outcomes. We believe that, as has happened with other empirical sciences, part of the maturation of the social sciences will be a growing dissatisfaction with predictive success as the primary goal of analysis. Predicting 90% of the variance will not be enough if we have no real idea about the mechanisms that relate the independent and dependent variables. Even putting aside the problem of spurious relationships, predictive accuracy alone tells us far less about real-world processes than we sometimes suppose.

We are not saying that other formal languages cannot be used to deal with uncertainty, counterfactuals, or process. We argue only that these forms of analysis often require one to relax simplifying assumptions and that mathematical models quickly become intractable. In mathematical modeling, one uses algebraic manipulation to find closed-form solutions, which must completely disentangle the formal definitions of all variables and parameters so that each can be expressed, alone on the left side of the equation, as a function of other variables and parameters. Computational modeling, on the other hand, specifies all formal relationships algorithmically and discovers solutions by "running" the algorithms, that is, by computing the particular solutions for a range of initial conditions. Mathematical modelers deal with algebraic intractability by systematically relaxing one assumption at a time, thereby maintaining solvability. Although this is a very useful mode of analysis, it does not allow one to deal with the complex interactions that may occur when one relaxes several assumptions simultaneously. The bottom line is that computational modeling allows us to represent more complex structures and processes without losing important analytic focus.

Throughout this discussion, we have emphasized the top-down role of theory in providing testable predictions and "imposing order" on an unruly world, while generally ignoring the equally important bottom-up role of empirical analysis in providing many of our initial ideas and "imposing truth" on headstrong theory. Empirical modeling techniques have become far more sophisticated in recent years, so that relatively complex processes now can be represented. Computational modeling allows still greater complexity than purely empirical modeling, which is limited by the need for convergence and optimization. Moreover, computational models can help us bridge gaps in data, which can be a problem for empiricists. For exactly these reasons, computational methods such as genetic algorithms already are being used by some empirical modelers to allow them to deal with more detailed processes. In addition, one can induce theory from empirical work, represent this theory as a computational model, and generate new predictions from the model. We would be far from the first to suggest that scientific progress depends on this sort of interplay.

There are several reasons to model computationally. First, these methods allow us to combine the rich detail of qualitative research with the rigor of quantitative and formal research. Second, computational models can represent complex theoretical structures without ignoring process validity. In this monograph, we hope to convince you that computational modeling can be very helpful, and sometimes is essential, for theory development in the social sciences. Some areas of social research will benefit more than others, and the particular computational tools used will differ based on the questions asked. "Tailor the model to the research question, not vice versa" is still a useful aphorism (Fiorina, 1975, p. 148).

Where Is Computational Modeling
Likely to Be Most Useful?

To facilitate discussion of this question, we have created a three-dimensional taxonomy of social science research based on the degree of simplification, the level of analysis, and the time scale of model processes. This organizational scheme focuses on the choices researchers make when studying real-world processes. For example, a cultural anthropologist may choose to study western African socialization using a complex typology, at the level of family units, and focusing on processes on an intergenerational time scale. Figure 1.1 depicts this taxonomy, collapsed to the two most important dimensions.

We have dubbed the horizontal axis in Figure 1.1 Occam's dimension based on his call for reducing a problem to its core features. This continuum ranges from highly simplified bivariate relations to the rich buzzing welter of the unanalyzed world. Although simplification is a ubiquitous goal of science, taken to extremes it can lead to misunderstanding of influences and processes, so the degree of simplification is an important research choice. Even Occam applied his razor carefully, and only to features of nature that safely could be ignored. He argued that every concept or process that is important to a theory must be included in a valid model of that theory. In the words of Albert Einstein, "Everything should be made as simple as possible, but not simpler."

The vertical axis of Figure 1.1 represents our second dimension, the level of analysis. It ranges from micro to macro, from intra-individual to global. We should emphasize here that we are agnostic in the debate concerning level of analysis: We do not argue that some basic level of explanation exists for behavioral analyses, to which all theories must reduce. It should be clear from our earlier discussion, however, that we value process validity highly. The appropriate level of analysis for a given theoretical model depends on the causal process being modeled. Like degree of parsimony, the unit of analysis in research is a theoretical choice that should be made carefully based on the processes of interest.

Our third dimension (not portrayed in Figure 1.1) is the time frame of analysis. This ranges from the examination of nearly instantaneous processes, such as cognitive reaction time studies measured in milliseconds, to epochal phenomena such as societal and cultural evolution. Although there is some practical correlation between this dimension and the level of analysis—neurological processes operate almost instantaneously, while we usually study only the ponderous movements of global systems—they

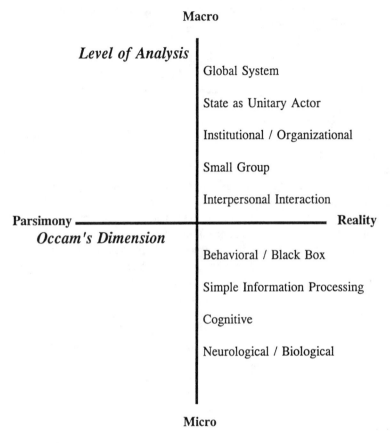

Figure 1.1. Typology of Models in the Social Sciences

become clearly distinct choices as we move toward the centers of both dimensions, and they are logically independent.

Four issues related to this simple typology direct us to areas of social science research in which computational models will be useful. First, the fundamental prerequisite for any formal model, computational or mathematical, is some degree of theory about the empirical process of interest. Several areas of research probably lack the necessary theoretical knowledge to support a computational modeling project. Subdisciplines that remain very traditional and nonrigorous, which tend to lie at the "reality" end of Occam's dimension, are least likely to have the necessary theoretical infrastructure. On the other hand, we have pointed out that the flexibility of computational models makes them more tolerant of theoretical uncertainty than other formal methods and that they can join the rigor of quantitative with the richness of qualitative analysis. Computational modeling can be used to "push the envelope" of theoretical knowledge in areas where traditional research has accumulated vast quantities of rich, possibly unquantified data. In fact, some of the social scientists most interested in computational modeling are in areas such as foreign policy analysis and cultural anthropology, subdisciplines that always have been suspicious of simplification, believing that the real-world systems they study are fundamentally complex.

Second, the advantage of computational over mathematical modeling is clear when the latter becomes intractable as a result of complexity. Many theories, however, are in fact parsimonious, and for these theories mathematical analysis may be more appropriate. If useful knowledge about an empirical process is captured in a simple theory, so much the better.

Third, one of the most difficult problems that scientists face as process knowledge becomes more detailed is that empirical measurement becomes less direct. For example, some dismiss cognitive processes as "unobservable" and "unresearchable" because we cannot directly measure changes in cognitive variables (e.g., attitudes). In fact, most factors hypothesized to affect social processes are measured indirectly. The problem is that the subjective assessment of the directness of measurement depends on the quality of the measurement theory and on how "tangible" the connections between measurement and concept seem. The quality of such empirical links appears to weaken as we move toward the extremes of both the level-of-analysis and time frame dimensions. Thus, to be tested, theories of human cognition and global systems each require complex measurement assumptions; the processes at both extreme levels seem intangibly connected to observable factors.

Computational methods offer two kinds of help here. First, they are less constrained by reality in the sense that complex counterfactuals can be tested within a validated computational model. We can posit several competing conceptions of unobservable processes and test their implications. (We are not saying that other methods are incapable of counterfactual analysis, only that such analyses are likely to be quite complex and potentially intractable.) Taber and Steenbergen (1995), for example, do this to contrast the implications of 10 decision rules that people might use when evaluating political candidates. Second, many techniques, bordering on computational modeling, have been developed by empiricists to test complex measurement theories (Bollen, 1989). These statistical methods—"auxiliary computational models"—enable us to test more complex theories toward the extremes of both the level-of-analysis and time frame dimensions.

Finally, scientists who seek theoretical synthesis may find computational methods useful. Bits and pieces of formal theory or empirical findings exist for many social processes. Hybrid theory that brings together various related speculations about some aspect of behavior often is helpful, although complex. A computational model may help us link together the disparate pieces and analyze their combined effects. One of the most important types of synthetic theory seeks ways to cross levels of analysis. Some theorists would like to model aggregate behavior as the combined behavior of the constituent individual actors. This undoubtedly is more than a simple "summation," because interactive effects may lead to emergent properties for the overall system and properties of the system may condition individual behavior. Hybrid, multilevel theory sometimes may be very complex, making computational methods such as dynamic simulation, cellular automata, and genetic algorithms very attractive.

In sum, we believe that computational models will have their greatest impact on social science research for which some lower threshold of process theory exists but mathematical and statistical methods are intractable, where measurement seems less direct, and where one wishes to gather theoretical pieces into an integrative whole. In terms of our typology, the greatest contributions will be made toward the middle of Occam's dimension, but pushing the "reality envelope," toward the extremes of the level-of-analysis and time frame dimensions, and wherever theoretical synthesis seems desirable but unattainable using other methods.

Drawbacks of Computational Modeling

We have argued that computational modeling shares many of the important merits of both quantitative and qualitative methods. With so much going for it, one could wonder why it is not the method of choice in the social sciences. The fact is that computational modeling cannot replace current techniques but can only augment them. There are drawbacks to its use.

First, we must distinguish myth from fact, as several misconceptions persist. Many believe, for example, that these are extremely arcane methods, best left to the "experts." As in many misconceptions, there is a grain of truth (and not too long ago, it was indisputable). Computational modeling is a method not unlike those that researchers already are comfortable with, such as statistical analysis, survey research, experimentation, case study, and mathematical modeling. Although these once presented a steep learning curve, once the basics were mastered, the benefits became obvious. As is true for each of these other methods, there are many degrees of computational modeling. Modern spreadsheet programs and statistical packages are useful platforms for some dynamic simulation. Other computational methods can be programmed using special software packages called shells, which can insulate users from the most technically difficult work. Moreover, because of the prevalence of computers in colleges and high schools, an increasing number of entering graduate students already have general programming skills. In addition, opportunities continue to increase for collaboration with experienced programmers. (In our experience, computer scientists usually are enthusiastic about social science problems.) In short, computational methods are tools to be learned like any other. How deeply one delves should depend on the degree of power and flexibility needed to apply the tools to one's substantive research agenda.

A second misconception is that there is little payoff for the effort of learning this "new" methodology. Some point to the dearth of computational publications in the social sciences, although articles continue to appear in the major journals, with the trend indicating more to come. As with all methods, the bottom line is utilitarian: Computational work that focuses on important substantive problems, uses appropriate tools, finds appropriate empirical tests, and generates interesting results will gain attention.

Several drawbacks are more real. First, a danger exists from undisciplined computational modeling. The problem is that although we focus in this slim introduction on the technical aspects of computational modeling, research must be guided by substantive knowledge. As the old computer adage goes, "garbage in, garbage out." Unfortunately, those with the technical sophistication to use computational modeling may lack the substantive knowledge necessary to design and test a useful computational model, while experts in the substantive field may not have the necessary technical ability.

If the greatest advantage of computational modeling is that it facilitates complex process models, the greatest drawback is the difficulty in testing process validity. This issue is important enough to warrant extended discussion in Chapter 5, where we address model validation. For now, we simply point out that this problem is not limited to computational modeling. Any attempt to build theory that explains rather than simply predicts will face the difficulty of assessing process validity.

General Stages in a
Computational Modeling Project

Earlier, we described three phases of a computational modeling project: developing a process theory, expressing the theory as a computer program, and simulating the theory by running the program. Before discussing particular tools and methods of evaluation, it might be useful to provide readers with a clearer understanding of the "life cycle" of an idealized project. Figure 1.2 depicts this mythical creature as a sequence of four general phases: theory development, model development, model evaluation, and refinement. Keep in mind that an actual project will likely be messier than this simplified overview.

Theory Development

Lave and March (1993) provide an invaluable lesson by beginning their primer on modeling with "an introduction to speculation." The genesis of any good modeling project is some observation or question that piques one's curiosity. Sometimes, as with most of Lave and March's examples, the observation is a simple empirical regularity, and the question asks for a simple process explanation, which ideally draws on existing theory. Sometimes, as with most of the examples in this book, the observation is more complicated, perhaps taking the form of dissatisfaction with existing theoretical explanations of some complex phenomenon. The issue then becomes how we can fashion existing theoretical ideas and novel hypotheses into a more satisfying explanation.

Obviously, theory development cannot occur in a vacuum. One needs a solid grasp of existing substantive knowledge and theory about the research domain. Too often, researchers become committed to particular analytic tools, such as computational modeling, and lose sight of the substantive questions. This stage of the project, then, often requires original empirical analysis and careful review of the relevant empirical and theoretical literatures. Although replication too often is not performed in the social sciences, it should be employed intentionally rather than by accident.

In the social sciences, this period of study is likely to reveal one (or possibly a combination) of several cases: (a) a simple, elegant theory, possibly already expressed as a mathematical process model, that appears

14

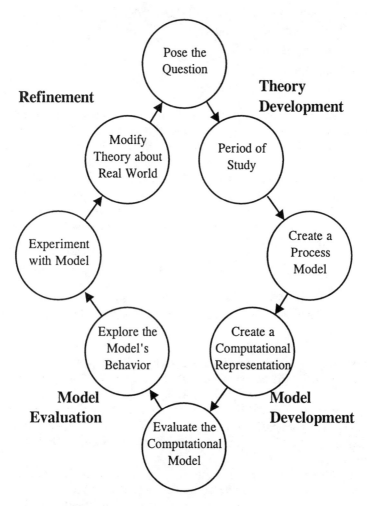

Refinement

Pose the
Question

**Theory
Development**

Modify
Theory about
Real World

Period of
Study

Experiment
with Model

Create a
Process
Model

Explore the
Model's
Behavior

Create a
Computational
Representation

**Model
Evaluation**

Evaluate the
Computational
Model

**Model
Development**

Figure 1.2. Stages of Computer Modeling

to explain the original observation; (b) a reasonable, though underdeveloped, general theory that offers a promising explanation but that has seemed too complex for formal analysis; (c) a variety of unconnected theoretical snippets (perhaps expressed as mathematical process models), many of which find some empirical support but none of which seems capable of explaining the observation alone; (d) many separate quantitative empirical results, perhaps generated by "black box" models, none of which are capable of explaining the observation; or (e) many rich qualitative studies, with little attempt at developing rigorous theory, perhaps because the underlying processes intuitively seem to be too complex for existing theory-building tools. In all but the first case, a computational modeling project may be appropriate and helpful. Theory must be adopted, adapted, or created at this point, but this process is well beyond our scope in this monograph.

Model Development

Developing a model presumes the existence of theory (which in our loose usage includes theoretical hunches and what might be called pretheory). For computational modeling, this stage divides into two parts: building a process model and expressing that model as a computer program. From unfortunate experience, we know that a great deal of effort can be wasted by trying to code a computational model prematurely.

The first step should be to create a process model of the theory. Usually, we begin by explicitly identifying the important variables and concepts. It helps to create an inventory of concepts on paper when dealing with a complex model. This "concept inventory" should define all variables and parameters in qualitative terms (perhaps with a loose notion of how they might be operationalized) and describe, when appropriate, their quantitative features (e.g., is a variable continuous, or does it assume discrete values? Does it adopt values only in particular ranges?). We then roughly frame the overall process (again, on paper), beginning with a black box model that only identifies input and output variables, then moving to intervening factors. Finally, it is useful to develop detailed flowcharts of these processes and, when possible, of subprocesses. Important decisions that bear on model evaluation (Chapter 5) are made while building the model. The level of parsimony, for example, must be decided at this stage.

Once a process model exists on paper, one is ready to choose a modeling method or set of methods. Assuming that the model is too complex for the algebraic manipulations necessary to achieve closed-form solutions, computational methods will be needed. One should try to choose the computational language that most naturally expresses the concepts and processes in the model. Once the appropriate technique is chosen, the computational representation finally can be created. Again, it often is useful to create a more detailed flowchart at this point to maintain focus and clarity in the actual programming task. Remember that one needs a complete algorithmic description of the model for it to work. When the theory does not specify a link in the overall process flow, guesses must be made. These may be competing theoretical explanations of the subprocess, or they might be relatively theory-neutral. In the latter case, empirical analysis might provide enough information to guess the distributional effects of the missing subprocess, which can be functionally implemented using random variables.

Model Evaluation

Before experimenting with a model, one must thoroughly "debug" the program. One must ensure that no errors were introduced when translating the process model into the computational representation. The first stage of model evaluation examines the degree of correspondence between the model and its covering theory, which is called its internal validity.

Once one is content with a model's internal validity, its external validity should be tested. The stages of evaluation will be described more fully in Chapter 5, so we will limit our discussion here to a brief list of our main points. The general standards for evaluating any model are Truth, Beauty, and Justice, with the most important being Truth. The standards for Truth divide into internal validity, outcome validity, and (in many cases) process validity. A model's outcome validity can be tested by comparing its predictions with real-world data and with the predictions of other competing models. Finally, process validity can be assessed through face validity, testing of assumptions, and multilevel outcome validation.

If the model passes initial evaluation, we are ready to explore its behavior. This may include running experiments within the simulated theoretical world, and it may include counterfactual analysis, which allows researchers to address what might happen if the world were different from observation but still followed the theorized processes. Both types of analysis increase the range of speculation available to social scientists. Model evaluation continues throughout this process as we assess each of the model's implications. Those that confirm existing scientific knowledge add confidence in the model's validity; those that challenge it should be tested empirically, for either we have learned something new about the world or there is something wrong with the model.

Refinement

We discuss theory and model refinement last, but Figure 1.2 in fact chases its tail through these phases; the growth of theoretical understanding is an ongoing process. Depending on what has been learned from model evaluation, one may modify or discard either the theory or the model. When a model is a good expression of the theory (i.e., it is internally valid), it implicates the theory in its successes and failures. If the model is a looser interpretation of the theory, its failures may not pertain to the theory. This latter situation should be avoided, because it leaves one in the precarious position of not knowing whether the model's implications, which have taken so much effort to discover, tell us anything about the theory and its explanatory power for the original question.

When the predictions of an internally valid model are not borne out, the assumptions and processes of the theory may be refined or the theory may be discarded. In either case, we return to the initial questioning stage armed with new, possibly helpful information. We know that the original theory is unsatisfactory, and we may have some clues to why it is so. We should now understand why the model (and thus the theory) performed as it did, and this may suggest a direction for theory change. Ideally, each cycle through these analytic stages will provide additional understanding, as our theories become richer and our models more precise.

An Overview of the Following Chapters

Computational modeling has a surprisingly long history in the social sciences, with research examples from the infancy of the computer revolution (e.g., Abelson & Carroll, 1965; McPhee, 1963). Over the past two decades, at an accelerating pace, the tools of computational modeling have become more sophisticated and diverse. Chapters 2 through 4 provide an overview of current methods, from traditional computer simulation through the more recent developments in cognitive science and machine learning. We will describe each method in turn and provide citations for those interested in delving more deeply. In addition, four extended illustrations should help put the methods in substantive context. Finally, Chapter 5 discusses the thorny problem of validating computational models. Throughout the monograph, we try to minimize jargon, but specialized concepts sometimes cannot be avoided. A glossary of all terms that appear in bold type can be found in the Appendix.

2. DYNAMIC SIMULATION MODELS

The earliest computer models in the social sciences were simulations of dynamic systems, including urban systems (Forrester, 1969), the global population (Meadows, Meadows, Randers, & Behrens, 1972), and electoral systems (McPhee, 1963). **Dynamic simulation** is the process of constructing a mathematical model of some real-world system and analyzing its behavior through computer-based experiments. It is worth noting that all the computational methods we discuss can be seen as special cases of dynamic simulation. The distinctive use of the term, however, pertains to explicitly numerical models of a dynamic system, while the specialized methods presented in following chapters tend to use other formalisms. In part because of the availability of special simulation software (e.g., STELLA or GPSS), dynamic simulation remains one of the most popular and productive computational methods.

Cellular automata are a specific class of dynamic simulation based on the metaphor of simple cellular interaction and reproduction. They were first proposed by John von Neumann in the 1940s and have applications in models that emphasize the interaction of social actors (e.g., individuals or nations).

In this and following chapters, we will treat each method at a logical level and rarely discuss programming, but a few words on the available programming tools may be helpful. Four types of programming environments exist: (a) general-purpose programming languages (e.g., BASIC, PASCAL, and C), (b) general-purpose software packages that include some programming capabilities (e.g., commercial spreadsheet or statistical software), (c) special-purpose programming languages (e.g., STELLA, GPSS, and SIMULA for dynamic simulation; LISP and Prolog for AI methods), and (d) special-purpose simulation packages or shells (e.g., MATLAB for dynamic simulation and EXSYS for AI methods). Flexibility is greatest and cost is lowest with general-purpose languages, but virtually all functions must be programmed. Simulation languages or packages contain extensive function libraries and are very easy to use, but they are less flexible and more costly. The sources we cite at the end of each method description contain more detail on these programming options.

Dynamic Simulation

As noted, dynamic simulation refers to the construction of and experimentation with a computerized model of a dynamic system. For example, to save time and money, an aeronautics engineer might design a computer model of a new wing design and simulate its performance under a range of conditions. Similarly, a sociologist might study the turf wars of inner-city gangs by experimenting with a computer model of the important processes. In both cases, computer simulation makes practical sense: The engineer saves time and money; the sociologist gains experimental control and the ability to manipulate the theoretical world.

In dynamic simulation, we usually are interested in the final values and time histories of particular numerical variables, called **state variables**, given a set of **initial values** for the state variables and parameters (Huckfeldt, Kohfeld, & Likens, 1982). This form of analysis is similar to running controlled experiments with the real-world system. For several reasons, it may not be possible to directly manipulate or control the real system. To achieve our research goal, we design a mathematical model that defines the relationships among the independent variables (control parameters and intervening variables) and the dependent variables (state variables, which themselves are likely to be intervening independent variables for other dependent variables). The set of **state equations** completely defines be-havior in the system; once parameters are set, the system of equations (or algorithms) may be "run" to determine outcomes and time paths to the outcomes. If the computerized model is a reasonable representation of the real system, we may learn about the real system by examining the simula-tion runs. This essentially is standard **numerical analysis**, done systemati-cally on computers.

As in all modeling, dynamic simulation requires that a number of choices be made. First, will the simulation be deterministic (as implied in the last paragraph) or stochastic? Deterministic models are easier to analyze and require only one simulation run per set of initial conditions. Some prob-lems, however, especially in the social sciences, seem inherently prob-abilistic, requiring the model to incorporate some representation of distributional behavior (possibly even "truly random" behavior). In the simulation literature, these are often called **Monte Carlo methods**, a term derived from the code name for the computer simulation of neutron diffusion as part of the World War II atom bomb project (Hoover & Perry, 1990). Whicker and Sigelman (1991, p. 41) remind us that one must include stochastic components only if the probabilistic factors interact with other important model variables. If they are additive components (i.e., noninteractive), their behavior should be represented by some measure of central tendency, because a fully stochastic representation will introduce sampling noise without adding usefully to the behavior of the model.

Analyzing a stochastic model requires multiple runs for every set of initial conditions, and one must report at least descriptive statistics when presenting results. When using certain distributions to represent the probabilism of the real-world system, such as the normal or uniform distributions, it may suffice to report average outcomes on state variables. If model histories (i.e., how these outcomes were generated) also are important, analysis will be far more complex. It may be necessary to define qualitatively distinct classes of behavior paths in the model and to analyze the distribution of model histories in these terms. For example, in a simulation of the decision whether to increase, maintain, or reduce arms levels in a two-nation competitive interaction, Taber (1993) described his results in terms of a simple typology of possible model behavior paths: an arms race, a disarmament race, a diverging race, or a stable, nonescalatory balance. Because the simulation was highly stochastic, each run was different, but each fell into one of these four qualitatively distinct categories.

A second choice concerns whether the model will incorporate continuous or discrete variables. Most important is how the variables change with time: If they vary continuously with time, state variables will be defined by differential equations; if they vary with discrete steps in time, difference equations are appropriate. It may also be that the real or theoretical system being modeled requires important discontinuities in otherwise continuous state equations. For example, prospect theory, a model of individual choice designed to account for deviations from rational choice theory, suggests that people tend to overweight subjectively the probability of very unlikely events (e.g., winning a lottery or casting the deciding vote in an election). Below some idiosyncratic threshold, however, all probabilities are subjectively experienced as zero, requiring a probability weighting function that jumps discontinuously to zero for probabilities below this threshold (Kahneman & Tversky, 1979). A simulation of individual choice based on prospect theory will use such a discontinuous weighting function.

Prospect theory, like many other models from the social sciences, contains nonlinear equations. Whether a simulation model represents linear or nonlinear processes is also an important modeling choice. In general, a linear system satisfies two conditions, called the "superposition property": (a) multiplying a system's input by a constant factor produces system output multiplied by the same factor, and (b) system output from all inputs applied simultaneously is the sum of the outputs produced from all inputs applied separately. Systems that do not satisfy the superposition property are nonlinear and should be modeled by linear state equations only as an intentional simplification.

For more detailed introductions to dynamic simulation, we recommend Kheir (1988), Hoover and Perry (1990), Whicker and Sigelman (1991), and Hannon and Ruth (1994). Garson (1994) provides a nice review of social science applications.

An Extended Example:
Bendor and Moe (1985)

Jonathan Bendor and Terry Moe (1985) provide a nice example of dynamic simulation, tackling an important problem that was not accessible to other formal methods, building a process model, and generating interesting and novel findings through systematic simulation. The theory they model concerns the interactions of business groups, consumers, government bureaucrats, and legislators in U.S. politics. They are interested in how these complex interactions affect bureaucratic budgets and levels of regulatory enforcement, and in whether any of these groups exerts disproportionate influence.

Bendor and Moe begin with the observation that the two most powerful, fertile, and predictively successful models of the behavior of governmental bureaucracies—Peltzman's (1976) theory of regulatory behavior and Niskanen's (1975) theory of budgetary policy—are limited by five important simplifications, each of which is empirically unreasonable: (a) both theories ignore important interactions, either combining actors that clearly behave strategically toward each other (such as bureaucrats and legislators, who are treated as a single actor in Peltzman's theory) or completely ignoring groups that are important actors in the process of interest (as public interest groups and consumers are ignored in Niskanen's model); (b) both treat the actors as unitary, so that the divisions within the legislature, for example, are ignored; (c) both are static; (d) both assume that all actors are able to calculate optimal outcomes; and (e) both assume perfect information (Niskanen only assumes that the bureaucracy is perfectly informed). Without these simplifications, early formal models of the theory became intractable, but because the assumptions structure our understanding of the processes at work and determine our theoretical and normative conclusions, Bendor and Moe thought it important to find out how much things would change if the limiting assumptions were relaxed. (Some mathematical work has relaxed these assumptions since 1985, though never all of them at the same time.) This required them to consider a different analytic framework, and they developed a dynamic simulation that relaxes, to varying degrees, all five assumptions.

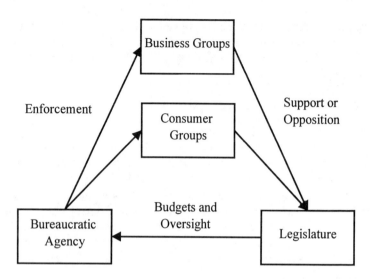

Figure 2.1. Bendor and Moe's Model

Their model has four central components (see Figure 2.1): (a) a bureau-cratic agency motivated to achieve higher budgets, reduced legislative oversight, or particular policy goals; (b) a legislature with 101 members, each interested only in reelection; (c) a consumer group that benefits from the agency's regulatory program; and (d) a business group that is hurt by regulation. Each group can take certain limited actions to achieve its goals: The agency controls the fraction of its budget spent on regulatory enforce-ment (called efficiency), the legislature (an aggregation of the 101 individ-ual legislators) sets the agency's overall budget and exerts oversight over the agency, and the two interest groups can support or oppose particular legislators based on their behavior toward the agency. As Bendor and Moe describe the model,

> In broad outline, the model is designed to reflect the circular flow of influence characteristic of representative government. Citizens pressure legislators through elections, legislators influence the bureau through budgets and oversight, the bureau affects citizens through the costs and benefits generated by regulatory enforcement—and the circle is closed when citizens link their electoral support to legislators' positions on agency-relevant issues. (1985, p. 757)

The model represents each of these process relationships as mathematical equations (the state equations), the forms of which are based on empirical findings and theoretical expectations about the motivations and limited adaptability of the actors.

Each legislator decides at the beginning of a model cycle whether to vote to increase or reduce the agency's budget, basing his or her vote on how the public responded to the vote in the last cycle. Votes may range continuously from a 10% reduction to a 10% increase. For example, a legislator who voted to increase the budget by 3% in the last cycle and reaped substantial electoral support would raise his or her vote to $(3 + x)\%$, where x is a monotonically increasing function of the change in electoral support. The 101 votes are cast, and the budget is set at the level of the median vote. (Legislators also have limited oversight power—they can "hassle" inefficient agencies—though we will ignore that feature of the model.)

The agency receives the budget as input and decides what fraction of the budget to spend on enforcement (efficiency). Its utility for degrees of efficiency is a function of the size of the budget, the agency's desire for slack (the part of the budget not spent on enforcement), and its preferred level of enforcement (its policy goal). The calculation of utility balances the agency's desires with the evidence it has about what consumers and business groups think of its past levels of efficiency (they observe this only indirectly through the current budget allocation from the legislature). Like the legislators, the agency is adaptive, taking into account how its environment reacted to its behavior (efficiency) in the previous cycle.

Next, Bendor and Moe define the impact of this enforcement decision on costs for business and benefits for consumer groups. Business costs are theorized to increase at an increasing rate with regulation, and consumer benefits are assumed to increase at a decreasing rate with regulation, so that

$$\text{costs} = k1 \times \text{enforcement}^2 \qquad (2.1)$$

$$\text{benefits} = (k2 \times \text{enforcement}) - (k3 \times \text{enforcement}^2) \qquad (2.2)$$

where k1, k2, and k3 are positive parameters. (More complex versions of the model also consider a tax component, so that the value to consumers of regulation is their benefits minus the associated tax costs.) As enforcement levels rise, consumers and businesses devote more resources to the upcoming electoral battle:

$$\text{consumers' political resources} = k4 + (k5 \times \text{benefits}) \qquad (2.3)$$

$$\text{businesses' political resources} = k6 + (k7 \times \text{costs}) \qquad (2.4)$$

where all the ks are positive parameters. The more that consumers and firms are affected by regulation, the more resources (presumably time and money) they will contribute to political action. Note that they cannot directly affect the agency in this model but must aim their political action at the elected legislators. Legislators who voted for budget increases gain the support of consumers, with the amount of support a function of how much they wanted to increase the budget in the last cycle. These legislators will not get the support of business, who favor legislators that voted to decrease the budget. The next cycle begins with the legislators once again considering their budget positions based on changes in their overall levels of electoral support.

Bendor and Moe did not test the model empirically, treating it as a purely formal exercise. Their analysis consisted of a classic experimental simulation, varying initial conditions and running the model until behavior "settled down" to some equilibrium pattern. Initial conditions, all dichotomous, included (a) whether the agency sought to maximize its budget, (b) whether the agency sought slack, (c) whether the agency sought a particular policy position (to favor consumers or business), (d) whether the legislature could exert oversight, (e) whether the actors adapted quickly or slowly, and (f) whether the first move of the legislature was to increase or decrease the budget. They implemented these qualitatively described initial conditions by changing parameters on the utility function for the agency (conditions a through c), enabling or disabling the oversight function (condition d), manipulating parameters on the decision functions for all three actors (condition e), and setting the initial positions of the 101 legislators (condition f). Bendor and Moe varied these initial conditions in seven basic patterns (they did not examine all combinations in a full factorial design). They were interested in the final states (and time histories) of the state variables—budget level, enforcement level, efficiency, and levels of political action by business and consumers—given the seven patterns of initial conditions. To use a term familiar to all social scientists, these are their dependent variables.

The results of this simulation are interesting both because they strongly support an existing theoretical tradition, that of pluralism, and because they paint a far more detailed picture of the processes involved in bureaucratic politics than did earlier formal work. Although still a caricature, the model at least has recognizable features. The experimental variations of the model yielded three broad patterns of final states. First, a pluralist equilibrium, in which business and consumer resources are equal and all other important variables approach steady state values, tended to emerge when agencies were proconsumer, legislatures had oversight power, and agencies adapted more slowly than legislatures. Second, degenerate solutions, with huge, unspent regulatory budgets, emerged when proconsumer legislatures with no oversight power other than budgetary allocation encountered slack-seeking agencies. Third, a compromise solution, in which enforcement levels fluctuate between highly probusiness and the pluralist equilibrium, emerged when agencies favored business. The most striking result is the strong support for the pluralist model under a wide range of conditions.

Examining the time histories of the state variables, the model also supports descriptive accounts of regulatory decision making in which policy emerges in fits and starts, with frequent unintended consequences. It suggests that, contrary to the expectation of many critics of pluralism, relatively diffuse consumer groups may generally hold their own against well-organized business interests. Finally, the model yields at least one truly surprising result: Even a purely budget-maximizing agency (i.e., no other factors affect its utility function) pays attention to its environment. Given the theory expressed in this model—one of interaction among adaptive agents, who can get what they want only through indirect action— such agencies will not necessarily become bloated, unresponsive, and inefficient, as conventional wisdom often claims.

Bendor and Moe conclude their 1985 article by suggesting a variety of interesting variations on the model and its analyses. One of the most important benefits of a well-supported computational model is that it can be used experimentally to explore real-world or counterfactual situations that are not subject to experimental control. This model is a prime candidate for validity testing and further analysis along these lines.

Cellular Automata

Cellular automata (sometimes called lattice models) are a subset of dynamic simulations that model discrete dynamic systems of interacting units, where the units are very simple and the rules of interaction local (that is, interaction is limited to the immediate neighborhood of a cell). They may be used to model a variety of interactive, nonlinear systems—for example, migration or the spread of public opinion—in which system dynamics are complex or unpredictable (possibly chaotic) but the individual behavior driving the system is simple and easily described (Cowen & Miller, 1990; Haken, 1983). Cellular automata are spatial representations of interacting units or cells. In their simplest form, they might be drawn on a large piece of graph paper divided into many equal cells or, when too large to represent conveniently on paper, on "virtual" graph paper in computer memory. There is a finite set of states, any of which may describe a particular cell at a discrete point in time. In the simplest case, cells take on one of two values: They are on or off, Republican or Democrat, black or white. At each discrete step of the model, each cell computes its new state from the states of its neighbors, usually defined to be immediately bordering cells. For example, a cell might "flip" (change state) every time three of its four immediate, nondiagonal neighbors are in the other state.

A cellular automata, then, is defined by the number of cells, the possible cell states, a function defining which cells are neighbors, and a transition function for calculating new states based on the states of neighboring units. Each of these is open to the modeler's discretion, making cellular automata a particularly flexible computational method when the research problem fits the general form of the model.

Thomas Cusack and Richard Stoll (1990) provide a fascinating application of the cellular automata approach, modeling the realist theory of international politics. Although a complete description of their model, adapted from Bremer and Mihalka (1977), is beyond our scope, we can outline briefly its most salient features. The international system is represented as a collection of up to 98 states, where each state has territory (it "owns" some of the 98 cells in the total matrix), power, and basic preferences. Each iteration of the model includes five phases of behavior: (a) states face the possibility of internal war, which might lead to territorial disintegration into smaller collections of cells; (b) states may choose to initiate a dispute with one of their neighbors, perhaps to seize territory; (c) the dispute(s) may escalate or fizzle out, depending in part on alliance choices; (d) war may erupt from one or more of these disputes; and (e) power is adjusted to reflect the outcome of wars. Cusack and Stoll find, in part, that implausible conditions must exist to ensure stability in a realist system. Wars and expanding empires result unless stringent conditions are enforced, for example, that overwhelming power superiority is necessary for a reasonable expectation of winning a war. See Farmer, Toffoli, and Wolfram (1984), Rietman (1989), and Gutowitz (1991) for further information on cellular automata.

3. KNOWLEDGE-BASED SYSTEMS

Artificial intelligence (AI) is very hard to define coherently and as a consequence is poorly understood. Part of the difficulty lies in the diversity of AI methods, but the most fundamental reason is the diversity of AI goals. Coming out of at least five major academic disciplines—cognitive psychology, philosophy, linguistics, computer science, and engineering—AI means something different in each. The goals of AI divide roughly into three main areas: (a) the empirical and theoretical study of human knowledge and intelligence (individually, in groups, or in organizations), (b) the study of and attempt to build machine intelligence, and (c) the application of intelligent algorithms to the solving of practical problems (e.g., in business technology).

The first of these goals is of greatest interest to the readers of this monograph series, so we will focus on knowledge-based systems, including **semantic networks**, **frame systems**, **expert systems**, and **hybrid systems**. The particular tools that we present in this section are connected intimately to the research goals of cognitive and organizational science and cannot be discussed apart from the theoretical frameworks that produced them. In particular, all these methods share an assumption known as the **knowledge representation hypothesis** (Reichgelt, 1991): All intelligent processing is based on stored information, organized in such a way that it can be applied to the processing of new information. These stored information structures, called knowledge, play a causal role in the generation of human behavior. Given this assumption, the tools of cognitive science seek ways of iden- tifying empirically the knowledge people use, representing that knowl- edge in computational models, and studying the knowledge-based models to learn more about the real-world system. In this section, we will address the second task by describing a number of knowledge representation formalisms.

Semantic Networks

One of the oldest tenets of psychology, that knowledge is stored asso-ciatively in human long term memory, underlies **semantic networks**, a knowledge representation formalism introduced in Ross Quillian's doc-toral dissertation (1968). Semantic networks represent conceptual knowl-edge as a network of linked nodes—that is, directed graphs—in which the meanings of concepts are contained in the linkages among concept nodes. The types of nodes and links used in a particular semantic network—its

primitive structure—must be defined in the cognitive theory being modeled. The most important debate on the nature of primitives, which we will not discuss at length, concerns how semantics (i.e., concept meanings), are to be defined. At a minimum, one must be completely explicit about the meanings of the primitives in a particular semantic network model, though many computational modelers have been notoriously sloppy in defining their primitives.

One view, evident in the work of Quillian, defines conceptual knowledge as in a dictionary: Each dictionary entry (corresponding to a **type node** in the network) is defined in terms of other words (**token nodes**), which must themselves be looked up (by searching for the matching type nodes). For example, Marxism may be defined as "a system of thought developed by Karl Marx and Friedrich Engels claiming that historical change is the result of class struggle." This information would be represented in a semantic network by linking the type node "Marxism" to a set of token nodes for all the information in the definition. The token nodes in the definition are themselves defined elsewhere in the network, where they appear as type nodes (e.g., "class" might be defined in another part of the network as "a social or economic stratum sharing basic characteristics"). In Quillian's formulation, type nodes may be linked to tokens in five ways. First, a concept might be a subclass of another (SUBC), as newspapers are a subclass of the media. Second, a concept may modify another (MOD), so that a newspaper may be modified by the descriptor "local." Third and fourth, several nodes may be linked conjunctively (AND) or disjunctively (OR). Finally, Quillian allowed the relationship in a link to represent any verb connecting a subject and an object; for example, "the regional newspaper *owns* the local paper." Many other types of primitive links have been defined since Quillian, including the "instance of" link (INST), which allows knowledge to be represented about particular instances of a concept class (e.g., Ronald Reagan and Jimmy Carter are each instances of the concept "former president"), and the "is a" link (ISA), which also represents hierarchical knowledge, though somewhat sloppily because it fails to distinguish instances of a class from subclasses (e.g., Tweety ISA bird is not different in the formalism from bird ISA animal).

Consider the example in Figure 3.1, which shows a semantic network fragment for the information in the sentence, "The smiling politician kissed the crying baby." This particular politician, represented by the token node p21 (meaning that this is the 21st politician about whom knowledge is stored), is connected through an instance link to the type node "politician." Politician p21 is smiling, which is represented by a MOD link to the node

29

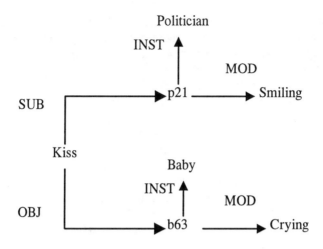

Figure 3.1. A Semantic Network Fragment

"smiling," and p21 is the subject of the verb node "kiss," which has as its object b63, an instance of a baby, modified by the node "crying." As in a dictionary, all the type nodes acquire their meanings through links to other nodes in the full network, not shown.

Defining semantics in this way is fundamentally circular. A dictionary is completely useless to someone who understands none of the words in it. That is, one must build up one's vocabulary from some primitive word concepts that already are known. It may not be enough to define primitive node and link types. This line of argument has been influential in semantic network modeling, leading some to define a set of semantic primitives that are assumed to be understood (e.g., "red" is assumed to be understood through visual sensory memories that can be recalled whenever the concept "red" is invoked). The most extreme version of this position is found in the work of Roger Schank (Schank & Abelson, 1977), whose conceptual dependency theory posits a very small number of semantic primitives to which all other meaning reduces.

To this point, we have described semantic networks as if they are static knowledge structures, but any useful knowledge representation formalism must also allow dynamic inferencing, that is, the generation of information not present in a stimulus by applying prior knowledge. Two inferencing mechanisms have been developed for semantic networks. The first, called **spreading activation**, is based on the assumption that nodes are differentially accessible. To account for this notion, links and/or nodes are indexed for their level of activation, where more active nodes, or nodes reachable through an activated path of links, are more accessible. In most models, this level of activation is interpreted as the degree to which the node or link has been energized by having been thought about. Three simple rules have been used to control the spread of activation through a network: (a) the exposure rule asserts that external stimuli (e.g., reading a newspaper headline) activate their matching nodes; (b) the fan rule says that activated nodes spread activation to directly linked nodes (or to the links themselves in some models), with the amount of activation spread a function of the activation levels of the nodes and links; and (c) activation decays through time unless maintained by reapplication of either of the first two rules. Spreading activation is used in some models to determine whether two nodes in a network are related. Called intersection search, this method spreads activation simultaneously from the two nodes through the network until the two search "fans" intersect at some node, or until all possible links have been traversed without intersection. If a common node is found, it may be used as a basis for semantic comparison of the two original nodes. The activation values of each node in the network at a given time (t) are a function of the activation levels of all linked nodes at the previous time (t − 1) plus an input that represents the activation value of the stimulus at time t.

The second inferencing process used in semantic nets, **inheritance**, is closely related to the representation of taxonomic knowledge. Modifying the classic example of Tweety the yellow bird, Figure 3.2 shows a fragment of a semantic hierarchy defining Ross Perot during the 1992 U.S. presidential campaign. Mr. Perot inherits the characteristics of the class of which he is an instance (politicians) and all higher classes of which politicians are a subclass. Using the process of inheritance to infer basic characteristics about a class member is often called **default reasoning**, because we assign the default values of the class or superclasses to particular instances. As we see in this example, however, we may override the default values with information stored with the instance. Because Ross Perot is identified explicitly as an independent, he is understood to be neither Republican nor Democrat, though these are the default values for politician in this hierarchy. We can infer that Mr. Perot is a two-eyed, two-legged independent.

An important issue in designing any inference mechanism is **control**, which refers to how decisions are made at each stage of an inference process. In the context of spreading activation, there are several options.

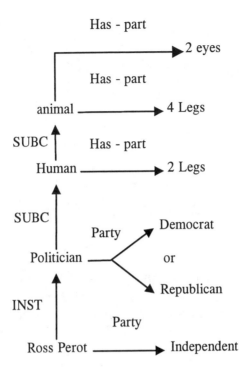

Figure 3.2. A Hierarchical Semantic Network

You can, for example, spread activation from a node according to the activation levels of the direct links or the nodes directly linked, as suggested in the fan rule. You also could spread activation equally to all linked nodes. In either case, you must still decide whether you will follow a depth-first or breadth-first control strategy, and you must decide when activation will stop spreading. Breadth-first search means that you activate all linked nodes one level out before spreading any activation to second-tier nodes. In other words, activation "fans out" from the original node. Depth-first search spreads activation from a node along a single path to its endpoint before spreading any activation along other paths from the original node. This method usually follows the most activated path first, so that at each node you move to the strongest linked node that has not yet been traversed. If there is no stopping rule—that is, activation will spread throughout the network until all possible paths have been traversed—the two methods generate the same information (though in different order). If instead the spread of activation weakens through time or through number of links traversed (as is the case in most cognitively plausible models), it can make a big difference in which information is inferred. Excellent discussions of semantic networks are found in Anderson (1983), Eysenck and Keane (1990), Findler (1979), and Reichgelt (1991).

An Extended Example:
Boynton and Lodge (1994)

G. Robert Boynton and Milton Lodge (1994) have developed a cognitive model of a political survey respondent, based on John Anderson's ACT* model (1983). The Boynton/Lodge model is designed to account for several troubling anomalies in the survey research literature, all of which suggest that respondents construct their responses to survey questions at the time of answering rather than simply retrieving crystallized attitudes from memory.

Boynton and Lodge view a survey respondent as a repository of basic declarative knowledge about politics, one who answers political questions by sampling this declarative memory using the question as a cue. The particular considerations from memory that form the response are a function of the differential accessibility of items in long-term memory. Because accessibility changes through time, a respondent may produce different answers to the same question at different times, and because the question is used as an inferential cue, even slight changes in wording can produce different responses.

This, in a nutshell, is their theory of survey responding. They model this theory as (a) a long-term memory (LTM) containing declarative knowledge in the form of a semantic network and (b) a working memory (WM) storing input information and the considerations inferred about the inputs. These inferences are made about presented stimuli by spreading activation through the network from the nodes that correspond to the stimuli. For example, the stimulus "What do you think of Bill Clinton's views on capital punishment?" spreads activation from the Bill Clinton and capital punishment nodes, so that considerations linked to these nodes have a chance of being moved to WM. Nodes have a strength, distinct from their activation levels, and "remembering" is a function of both node strength and level of activation. The model "learns" by adding, removing, or changing the strengths of nodes and links. Unlike most semantic networks, the Boynton/Lodge model represents affective feelings as well as cognitive knowledge;

each node in the network contains both semantic and affective information. For example, the Bill Clinton node will have semantic content and a liking tally. The activation values of each node in the network at a given time (t) are a function of the activation levels of all linked nodes at the previous time (t − 1) plus an input that represents the activation value of the stimulus at time t. Formalizing this as a set of difference equations,

$$\text{act}_i(t) = c_{i1}\text{act}_1(t-1) + c_{i2}\text{act}_2(t-1) + \ldots + c_{ii}\text{act}_i(t-1) \qquad (3.1)$$
$$+ \ldots + c_{in}\text{act}_n(t-1) + u_i(t)$$

$$\text{aff}_i(t) = c_{i1}\text{aff}_1(t-1) + c_{i2}\text{aff}_2(t-1) + \ldots + c_{ii}\text{aff}_i(t-1) \qquad (3.2)$$
$$+ \ldots + c_{in}\text{aff}_n(t-1) + u_i(t)$$

for $i = 1$ to n, where n is the number of nodes in the network, $\text{act}_i(t)$ is the level of activation of the semantic content of node i at time t, $\text{aff}_i(t)$ is the level of activation of the affective content of node i at time t, c_{ij} is the strength of the directed link from node j to node i (equal to zero if there is no link), and $u_i(t)$ is the activation value of the input stimulus.

Self-referential links (the c_{ii}), which control the amount of activation a node spreads to itself (representing how effectively "attention" can be maintained on a given concept), are assigned constant values based on psychological experiments, so that all c_{ii} for semantic activation are equal to .01, and all c_{ii} for affective activation are equal to .5. This follows from fairly robust experimental findings that cognition is more fleeting than affect. All other directed links in the model (all c_{ij}) range from zero to one. They remain zero unless a single informational input mentions the semantic content of both nodes together. Particular survey respondents may not link Haiti and Somalia in their LTM, though they may have some knowledge of each. That is, their semantic networks would have the link from the Haiti node to the Somalia node, $c_{HS,}$ set equal to zero. On reading a survey question asking whether the respondent "believes that the Haiti situation is similar to the Somalia case," our respondent would link the two for the first time, represented in the model by making c_{HS} nonzero. This new value is computed as a function of the relative strengths of the linked nodes (as opposed to their levels of activation). Specifically, the new value of c_{ij} is the strength of node j divided by the sum of the strengths of all nodes connected to node i. For our example, the link from Haiti to Somalia would now be equal to the strength of the Somalia node divided by the sum of the strengths of all nodes linked to Haiti. (Note that the link from Somalia to Haiti will be a different value; in general, $c_{ij} \neq c_{ji}$.)

Like activation level, node strength is computed by a set of first-order difference equations:

$$nodestr_i(t) = b_i nodestr_i(t - 1) + u_i(t) \qquad (3.3)$$

where $nodestr_i(t)$ denotes the strength of node i at time t, $i = 1$ to n, b_i is a parameter for the strength of memory, and $u_i(t)$ is the strengthening value of the input at time t. Again based on generalized experimental findings, Boynton and Lodge set b_i equal to .9. This fairly large value makes forgetting relatively slow.

The model is designed to represent at least the simple processing of a respondent when asked survey questions about politics. A question provides input, which is translated by Boynton and Lodge into numerical values for the $u_i(t)$ and applied to the appropriate nodes in the network. By Equations 3.1, 3.2, and 3.3, these inputs will change the values for the strengths of the corresponding nodes, for the semantic activation for those nodes, and for the affective activation for those nodes. Activation spreads to other nodes according to Equations 3.1 and 3.2, and new values for all non-self-referential link coefficients are computed as described above. The values for the network after this iteration, and after subsequent iterations, give the model's account of the respondent's information processing in LTM. The more activated nodes may be brought into WM to form the model's response to the input.

Boynton and Lodge test the model's ability to perform the basic act of representative politics, that of candidate evaluation and selection. They elicited the political knowledge of a set of experimental subjects to form the initial semantic networks (for the empirical procedure, see Boynton & Lodge, 1994). They then presented information about two fictitious political candidates (nine pieces each), both to the model of each experimental subject and to each subject (so that 18 informational inputs were entered into the semantic network for each respondent, according to the mathematical procedure outlined above). The subjects then chose a preferred candidate, and the models of the subjects "chose" a preferred candidate (the candidate whose inputs generate the most positive affect). Boynton and Lodge report approximately the same predictive success for this model as for a variety of formal decision models from the voting literature, though under several other conditions their model outperforms other models.

Frame Systems

In some introductory treatments, **frame systems** are grouped with se-mantic networks because both are based on the interconnectivity of knowl-edge. Semantic networks emphasize the idea that knowledge is contained in the links among concept nodes. Frame systems retain that idea while adding the assumption that knowledge is stored in larger chunks (Minsky, 1975). The linked nodes of semantic networks give way to linked **frames**, each containing far more information than does a single concept node.

Like the information contained in all the token nodes linked to a par-ticular type node in a semantic network, a frame contains what is essentially an extended description of some object or concept. A frame system of social relations, for example, might contain a frame for the social categories "friend" and "acquaintance." The friend frame would contain general information about the class of people who are friends: people for whom we feel affection, people we hold in high esteem, people who help out when we need assistance, and people we know well. In the parlance of frame systems, these descriptions are called **slots**, each with a slot name and a slot filler (these are sometimes called attribute-value pairs).

Like most semantic networks, frame systems usually are organized hierarchically, distinguishing superclasses, subclasses, and instances. The general friend frame described above is a class-frame. If our knowledge were portrayed as frame systems, we would each have an instance-frame for our friend Bob, which would be linked to a general class-frame by an INST link, as in a semantic network (the specific slots in our Bob frames probably would be different, however). The class-frame "friend" also would be linked to a more general class-frame "social relation" by a SUBC link, and so on.

A useful, though not universally followed, convention orders the slots in a frame hierarchically, so that the most "useful" information is found near the top. Often, the pieces of information in a frame's slots are indexed according to their subjective truth value, so that those attributes that are true of all class members occupy the top slots, those that usually are true occupy the middle slots, and those that frequently are false are found near the bottom. For example, virtually all countries have armies (a top slot), most are United Nations members (a middle slot), some believe in democ-racy (a lower middle slot), and few have names beginning with the letter Q (a bottom slot, if important enough to list at all).

Complex frame systems allow many types of slots and frames; their primitives tend to be less narrowly defined by convention than was true for semantic networks. For this reason, frame systems are a bit more flexible, though it is even more important that the modeler be clear on the primitives used. We already have mentioned two common types of frames for objects: class and instance frames. Frames also may be used to represent actions or verbs (e.g., revolt), generalized events (e.g., revolutions), specific events or cases (e.g., the French Revolution), or sequences of expected behavior. This last type of frame, called a script in Schank and Abelson's (1977) influential cognitive model, represents prototypical situations such as eating in a restaurant. Scripts are similar to generalized events but contain sufficient information about the structure of the event and the things that typically occur to allow inferences about situational behavior (e.g., how to order from a menu).

The simplest and most prevalent type of slot is the attribute-value pair described above. We also can use slots to define the links among frames, so that the slot names define the link types and the fillers point to other frames. Slots may contain sets rather than singular attribute-value pairs; in this case, the filler will be either a set definition (e.g., membership functions) or will list all set members (i.e., an extensive definition of the set). A filler instead may contain a set of restrictions on permissible values. A frame describing a bride's clothing, for example, might not specify a particular type of shoes, though sneakers might be prohibited. Finally, slots may define procedures. This is an important extension in the expressibility of this representational language. Semantic networks typically contain only **declarative knowledge**—knowledge about the descriptive properties of concepts and objects. Frame systems, on the other hand, can also represent **procedural knowledge**—knowledge about how to do something, or about how some process works. Procedures often are attached to slots by allowing slot fillers to contain IF-THEN production rules. At a minimum, this allows conditional information; in some cases, the rules may contain detailed conditional descriptions of some procedure (e.g., imagine a detailed rule that defines kissing). A complete wedding frame system might have a slot defining various ways the bride and groom may kiss, depending on the nature of the wedding (and the nature of the groom's relationship with his new father-in-law). The production rule may define a procedure for updating the value of the filler based conditionally on other information in the frame system. For example, a wedding frame system could have a slot identifying the person who performs the wedding as a priest if the bride and groom are practicing Catholics, a rabbi if Jewish, a public magistrate if nonreligious, or a captain if the wedding is performed

37

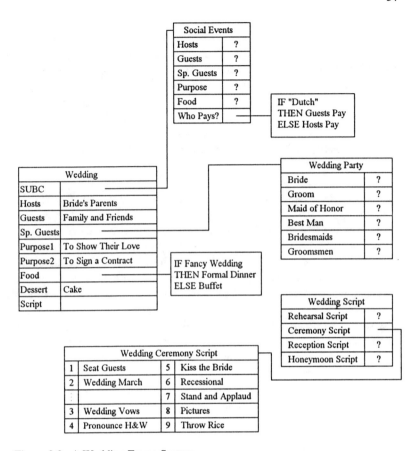

Figure 3.3. A Wedding Frame System

on a ship. In sum, the primitives for frame systems are both less tightly defined and more flexible than those for semantic networks.

Figure 3.3 gives an example of a frame system for a wedding, containing a description of the superclass (social events), a frame for the structure of a wedding, a frame identifying the wedding party, a wedding script broken into four components, and a frame for the ceremony part of the wedding script. In each frame, the slot names are listed down the left side, with the corresponding fillers listed down the right side. Many of the types of frames and slots, described above, are illustrated in this figure and need no further discussion.

Hierarchical organization, both of frame systems and of the slots within frames, facilitates the major inferencing mechanisms for frame systems—**matching** and **inheritance**. Inheritance and default reasoning work essentially as described for semantic networks and will only be illustrated here. Using Figure 3.3 as our example, weddings inherit the default properties of general social events unless these defaults are specifically overridden. We may infer, therefore, that the hosts—that is, the bride's parents—will pay for a traditional wedding, unless the particular wedding instance overrides the default.

Before inheritance can be used to infer new information, the appropriate frames must be selected from the overall knowledge base. The first step in a reasoning process using a frame system involves matching the (usually partial) description of input information with general frame descriptions, general scripts, or similar cases from the past stored as case frames, selecting the "best" (or most useful) stored knowledge. Consider a simple matcher, one that requires a perfect match between input information and frame, so that all input information must be present in the frame before it is invoked (though not all frame information must be present in the input). Observing a bride and groom might invoke (that is, activate) the wedding party frame in Figure 3.3 because all input information is present in the frame. Activating this frame allows the inference that a maid of honor and best man also are present. Further inferencing—for example, that the wedding party will have cake for dessert—might occur if the system contains inference mechanisms that pass activation backwards on "special guests" links. (This illustrates the point that one may, with caution, design all sorts of special-purpose inference processes for a particular frame system.) In some systems, even this simple matching mechanism may need more thought. If more than one frame matches all the input information, the system must decide which of the frames to invoke; the simplest control rule would invoke all frames that match perfectly, but this might create inference problems down the line, because inferences from these different frames may directly conflict. More complicated matchers are beyond our scope in this monograph but well worth further study (see Reichgelt, 1991; Winston, 1984).

Finally, unlike typical semantic networks, frame systems often explicitly represent uncertainty in knowledge. The degree to which the information in frames and slots is believed to be true may be indexed numerically, and inference mechanisms, both matching and inheritance, may be designed to operate on uncertainty. We will defer discussion of uncertain reasoning, however, to the section on expert systems.

Frame systems differ from semantic networks in that they (a) explicitly embrace the chunkiness of knowledge, making them natural representations for schema- or script-based models; (b) package declarative and procedural information together; and (c) explicitly represent uncertainty. As we have emphasized, the primitives of frame systems—syntactic and semantic—are less strictly defined and more flexible than those of semantic networks, which makes frame systems very expressive but potentially undisciplined (Reichgelt, 1991). However they differ, frame systems are fundamentally similar to semantic networks in the assumption of the interconnectivity of knowledge and the inference mechanisms that follow from that assumption. Frame systems have proven useful in representing analogical and metaphorical reasoning, as well as more general declarative knowledge.

We can illustrate frame-based systems with an application of the theory of **case-based reasoning** (Kolodner, 1992). Case-based reasoning is the process of understanding new experiences or situations by reference to similar cases from the past. In this view, people (and possibly organizations) store representations of each experience as a case-frame and interpret fresh experiences by invoking the appropriate case-frames. For obvious reasons, this approach has been very useful in highly constrained domains that rely heavily on precedent, such as choosing a favorite recipe or preparing a legal case.

HYPO is a frame-based model of legal reasoning designed to create an argument for a defendant (Rissland & Ashley, 1987). It contains a frame-based representation of a large number of legal cases that can be used as precedents for arguing new cases. HYPO proceeds in a series of steps: (a) the current case is analyzed along a set of dimensions that should describe its relevant features, (b) the frame-system is searched and a matching procedure used to identify similar cases, (c) these similar cases are retrieved (invoked), (d) they are categorized into those that support the defendant's position in the current case and those that do not, (e) the most "on-point" cases of each type are selected (again using a matching procedure), and (f) a "three-ply" argument is constructed, consisting of case arguments that support the defendant, case arguments that do not support the defendant, and counterarguments to the latter cases. Along the way, HYPO can identify the most serious legal problems for the defendant. Based entirely on prior cases stored as frames, retrieved according to a matcher, and processed according to specialized inference mechanisms, HYPO models the construction of a legal defense. Because case-based reasoning seems to be quite important for individuals and organizations (e.g., business firms often look to their specific past experiences to guide future policies), this theoretical position and the frame-based method should be quite useful for modeling a variety of social problems. For more information on frame systems, see Barr and Feigenbaum (1981), Reichgelt (1991), and Kolodner (1992, 1993). Slade (1994) provides one of the most sophisticated social science examples to date with his model VOTE.

Rule-Based Expert Systems

Production rules are the most popular knowledge representation language as well as the basis for the most prevalent product of AI—**expert systems**. Prior knowledge is expressed in production rule systems as sets of IF-THEN rules; the IF part is called the **antecedent** (or condition) and the THEN part is called the **consequent** (or action). Each rule contains the belief that the antecedent implies the consequent, though it does not necessarily follow that the antecedent causes the consequent. Unlike semantic networks or frame systems, rule-based systems represent knowledge as individual bits, which are connected only by the conditional implications of production rules.

For example, "cousin" might be expressed by the kinship rule

IF	{person1 is the son of person2} OR {person1 is the daughter of person2}
AND	{person2 is my uncle} OR {person2 is my aunt}
THEN	{person1 is my cousin}

This example illustrates an important feature of production rules: The antecedents (or the consequents) of rules may contain conjunctions and disjunctions of premises. Using Boolean logic, an antecedent is true when all of its conjunctive conditions are true. A disjunctive condition is true when one of its elements is true. Of course, as we discuss shortly, we are not limited to Boolean logic in computing truth values.

Rule-based models have three structural components: a **knowledge base**, a **working memory**, and an **inference engine** (or rule interpreter). The knowledge base contains the set of IF-THEN rules that the model will use to reason about input information. Working memory serves as a scratch pad for keeping track of initial conditions and all inferences that have been made. The inference engine contains processing mechanisms that combine the implicational beliefs in the knowledge base with the believed "facts" in working memory to produce new beliefs. These new beliefs are then added to the list of "known facts" in working memory.

Expert systems are rule-based or hybrid (i.e., using multiple representation formalisms together) systems that represent the specialized knowledge or beliefs of human experts in some limited domain. Because virtually all rule-based systems are expert systems, we will limit our discussion to this class of models. Expert systems have been built that mimic the behavior of geologists, medical doctors, auto mechanics, investigative reporters, mothers, statisticians, computer configuration engineers, and foreign policy decision makers, to name only a few of the thousands of applications that have appeared in the past 20 years. Most of these systems were built for the practical purposes of advising human decision makers or training novices when human experts are unavailable, unreliable, or too expensive. In many cases, these expert systems produce decisions or diagnoses indistinguishable from or better than those of humans in the relevant domain. Unlike humans, however, these systems are utterly unable to deal with decision problems outside their areas of expertise—they contain no "common sense" or other generalized knowledge. Indeed, this narrow specialization is both the major practical advantage and the major shortcoming of expert systems. For cognitive science, in which rule-based systems are used to model theories of human decision making, another problem is the purported "unnaturalness" of the language. Critics question whether humans actually represent knowledge mentally in rule-like pieces and whether their inference procedures resemble those described below (Eysenck & Keane, 1990).

Building an expert system involves three basic tasks: discovering the knowledge used by humans in the domain of interest, expressing that knowledge in a knowledge base, and designing an inference engine. The first task is empirical. One could interview or directly observe human experts as they solve domain problems, and using **knowledge engineering** techniques (Benfer, Brent, & Furbee, 1991; Pedersen, 1989), extract that knowledge, preferably as part of a formal coding process. Unfortunately, this process is often ad hoc, and although much has been written on knowledge engineering, little consensus has emerged. Most of the better work in the social sciences uses methods modified from the more general interviewing techniques developed in sociology and anthropology—what Benfer, Brent, and Furbee (1991, pp. 37-48) call "ethnoscience." These methods try to discover the basic concepts and categories, processes and theories, and questions and answers that experts use when thinking about the domain. In the next chapter, we will discuss ID3, a method for inducing rules directly from data that has become a standard tool for knowledge engineering.

Often in the social sciences, however, those whose knowledge or beliefs we model are not available for interviewing or direct observation. Political figures, for example, rarely welcome social scientists into their campaigns and tend to be suspicious of questionnaires. Making matters worse, their speeches or written policy statements will at best only imperfectly reflect their political beliefs, because they are written strategically, frequently by others. We believe that such sources should be used as indicators of a public figure's personal beliefs with great caution and only with express acknowledgment of their limitations. We have argued, however, that these sources, although indirect indicators of personal beliefs, may be more direct indicators of the shared beliefs in a given policy environment, which we call paradigms (Taber, 1992; Taber & Timpone, 1994b). Policymakers, in this argument, are advocates of a particular paradigm or shared belief system when they speak publicly and, if you are studying the paradigm, it does not matter whether they fully believe what they say. Content analysis techniques can be used to analyze documentary data (Weber, 1990). Like the interviewing methods mentioned above, this form of archival research seeks to discover the concepts and categories, processes and theories, and questions and answers used by domain experts.

The second task is to express the knowledge extracted from domain experts in the form of production rules, a process sometimes called **prototyping**. (As we will see, expert systems often use hybrid representations that go beyond simple rule bases.) Although seemingly a simple translation step, the process of moving from coding sheets to knowledge base can be very difficult and is always a potential source of bias and distortion. Fortunately, rule bases are simple lists, which are easily modified at any point in development by adding or deleting rules. Errors, if caught, are easily corrected. As a general principle, rule bases should be built slowly and in chunks of related rules, starting with concepts at the highest level. For example, an expert system to advise probation officers might start by expressing rules that affect recidivism rates—for example, IF {parolee returns to old associates} THEN {probability of crime relapse is high}. For the first prototype, all important beliefs related to recidivism would be cast as production rules. When enough of the prototype is in place to generate inferences (see the discussion of inference mechanisms below), it should be tested for **internal validity** and possibly **face validity**. Inferences made from the recidivism rule base can be presented to probation officers for their critique. In the ideal project, successive prototypes are built that provide incremental improvements over earlier ones. The particular failures of a prototype—for example, generation of inferences that are internally inconsistent or to which domain experts object—should guide further search through existing code sheets or new interviewing. In the best possible case, where the appropriate data exist, a prototype's predictions can be tested statistically. AI-MOMS, a model of the prenatal care decisions of pregnant women, was designed explicitly to account for regression results, and prototypes of the expert system were compared statistically to real data (Benfer, Brent, & Furbee, 1991).

The third task—designing an inference engine—is not completely distinct from prototyping, because an inference engine must exist in order to test prototypes. Moreover, the nature of the inference engine affects the inferences made during prototyping. The basic inference mechanism for rule-based systems is **inference chaining**: When a rule's antecedent condition exists in working memory, meaning that it is believed to be true, the rule's consequent condition is added to working memory, meaning that we now believe it to be true. In this case, we say that the rule "fired." AI-MOMS, for example, contains a rule (paraphrased here), IF {there is home support for a pregnant woman} THEN {she will seek prenatal care late} (Benfer, Brent, & Furbee, 1991, p. 4). If we place in working memory the information {there is home support for a pregnant woman}, we can infer that {she will seek prenatal care late} in her pregnancy. If AI-MOMS contained a further rule (which it may not), IF {she will seek prenatal care late} THEN {there is a greater risk of problems}, we might infer this conclusion as well. These two rules, firing in succession, form an inference chain. An inference chain explicitly presents all the steps in a line of reasoning.

Things are not really this simple. Several decisions must be made in building an inference engine, and these decisions should be guided by the nature of the domain and the research question. An inference engine's main job is to solve the basic control problem, that is, to decide which rule(s) will "fire" at each inference cycle. This involves matching (so appropriate rules are chosen) and selection (so the "best" of all the possible matching rules are chosen). Because modifying one link in an inference chain can alter the entire chain, this is important.

The first design decision is whether the engine will match the antecedent part of the rule, as in the examples above, or whether it will match the consequent part. The former control regime, called **forward chaining,** starts with "known facts" and attempts to infer what is implied by those facts. It seems to be the most natural way to represent data-driven reasoning: Observe conditions and figure out what follows from those conditions, given a set of prior beliefs. For example, a model of the national economy might be designed to take as input a set of current conditions and infer the overall current health or future performance of the economic system. It would apply stored knowledge to discover what these current conditions imply. Consider three naive rules from this hypothetical system:

R1: IF   {interest rates increase}
     THEN {demand will decline}

R2: IF   {demand will decline}
     THEN {productivity will decline}

R3: IF   {productivity increases} OR {demand declines}
     THEN {inflation will decline}

If current conditions include rising interest rates, we can forward chain on the first rule, inferring that demand will decline. This allows us to forward chain on the second rule, concluding that productivity will also decline. Because rule R3 requires only that one of the two premises be true, we also can forward chain on it, inferring that inflation will decline as the ultimate result of rising interest rates.

Backward chaining, on the other hand, starts with goals (target conditions) and tries to infer what conditions might lead to those goals. It seems to be the most natural way to represent strategic reasoning and is the most common control regime in practical expert systems (for example, geological systems that seek mineral deposits). Our hypothetical model of the national economy might take as input a set of goals and infer the particular conditions or policies most likely to achieve those goals. With the goal of reducing inflation, we can illustrate backward chaining on the three rules above. Checking the consequent parts of the three rules, we discover that rule R3's consequent matches our goal of declining inflation. Looking to the antecedent, we see that we must either increase productivity or reduce demand to achieve lower inflation. Firing backward on rule R3, we set these as subgoals and look for ways of achieving either of them. We find that one of these subgoals, reducing demand, is the consequent of rule R1; backward chaining on this rule, we discover that increasing interest rates will produce our ultimate goal. If we represented these rules as a decision tree, forward chaining would trace path(s) from initial conditions toward some terminal node(s), while backward chaining would move from a terminal node through paths to initial conditions.

At every step in building an inference chain, more than one rule might match conditions in working memory; in such cases, the inference engine must choose among them. We call all possible matches in a single "match-fire cycle" the conflict set. One might choose to exercise little control, allowing all possible rules to fire each cycle, so that many parallel inference chains grow (sometimes called breadth-first search). In this strategy, one would want only to prevent rules from applying twice to the same inference chain and would continue to cycle through the rule base until no new rules would fire. This approach is impractical for many applications, but it is a good way to discover all possible inference chains that can "grow" from an input. Another strategy, called textual order, simply selects the first match from the knowledge base without searching any further. In some cases, however, this would require the rules in the knowledge base to be ordered. If the knowledge base is divided into conceptual modules, so that all rules pertaining to a given subject are found together, textual order works better. A third approach is recency, which selects the rule from the conflict set that matches the most recent element in working memory. This leads the model to pursue a single line of reasoning until it fails, which makes it a form of depth-first search control. One might also prefer more specific over more general rules, in a control strategy called specificity. If a rule matches more information elements in working memory (because it has a more complex conditional structure), it is more specific. The rule IF {a} AND {b} THEN {c} is more specific than IF {a} THEN {c}. Finally, one might favor more certain over less certain conclusions. The inference engine will select those rules that will add the most strongly believed inference to working memory. To see this, however, we must discuss uncertain reasoning. (Recall that uncertainty often must be considered in frame systems as well.)

All conditions in a production rule carry some truth value (the same may be true for frame systems). In Boolean logic, such conditions would be either true or false, leaving no room for degrees of truth, but uncertainty is ubiquitous in human reasoning, and computational models based on knowledge or belief structures must find a way to represent this uncertainty. The best known method of representing uncertainty is probability theory. One could use Bayes' theorem, for example, to calculate the conditional probabilities that correspond to rule-based inferences. Unfortunately, one needs a lot of information about prior probabilities to use Bayes' theorem, and we rarely have this information in expert systems. Moreover, some of the rules of probability theory are highly counterintuitive to human reasoners. To the extent that expert systems seek to represent human reasoning, probability theory does not seem to be the best choice.

Several alternatives to probability theory have been proposed, including the CF method. In this approach, every element α in working memory has a **certainty factor** (CF) that measures the system's degree of belief $MB(\alpha)$ and disbelief $MD(\alpha)$ in the element, such that $CF(\alpha) = MB(\alpha) - MD(\alpha)$. $MB(\alpha)$ and $MD(\alpha)$ vary between 0 and 1, and $CF(\alpha)$ ranges from -1 to 1. $CF(\alpha) = 1$ means that the system is certain that α is true; $CF(\alpha) = 0$ means that the system is unsure; and $CF(\alpha) = -1$ means the system is certain that α is false. This seemingly odd method allows human experts to assess belief and disbelief as independent dimensions, which is not allowed by probability theory. The probability that an event will happen and the probability that it will not must sum to 1. Human experts frequently treat belief and disbelief as independent factors. An economist might believe that rising interest rates make economic health more likely, perhaps subjectively raising this probability from .5 to .8. The same economist might not believe that rising interest rates make not having economic health less likely, though probability theory would require this probability to drop from .5 to .2 if the complementary probability of having economic health rose from .5 to .8.

Typically, the CFs for input conditions or goals in an expert system are supplied by the user. Each rule R in the knowledge base also has a certainty factor CF(R), derived during knowledge acquisition. Consider a rule IF α THEN β with $CF(R_1) = .3$. The CF method calculates belief in a new inference $CF(\beta)$ as the product of the CFs for the rule R_1 and the antecedent condition α (assuming forward chaining). So if α exists in working memory with $CF(\alpha) = .6$, rule R_1 will fire and place β in working memory with $CF(\beta) = .18$. Consider now a more complex rule, IF $\{\{\alpha_1$ OR $\alpha_2\}$ AND $\alpha_3\}$ THEN β_1 with $CF(R_2) = .3$. Working memory contains the elements α_1, α_2, and α_3 with corresponding certainty factors $CF(\alpha_1) = .1$, $CF(\alpha_2) = .9$, and $CF(\alpha_3) = .5$. This method assigns the minimum CF from a conjunction and the maximum from a disjunction, preserving the intuition that all elements must be true if they are conjunctive but only one must be true if they are disjunctive. The "global CF" for the antecedent of rule R_2 is $\min(\max(.1, .9), .5) = .5$. Multiplying this CF by $CF(R_2)$, we infer β_1 with $CF(\beta_1) = .15$.

The CF method is related to another method for dealing with uncertainty in expert systems: fuzzy logic (Zadeh & Kacprzyk, 1992). The main advantage of fuzzy reasoning in expert systems is the quantification of verbal uncertainty. The basic notion is that indefinite concepts—such as tall, about 35, very angry, sort of attractive, smart, or very loud—are not well represented by the traditional application of crisp sets (in which elements are either members or not). Using a controversial example, consider a range of IQs {80, 90, 100, 110, 120, 130}. Where is "smart"? Crisp sets define a membership function such that a person is either smart (say, above 110) or not. Fuzzy sets allow partial set membership so that the membership function for smart can be defined as follows: {80/0, 90/.2, 100/.5, 110/.8, 120/1, 130/1}. This quantifies smart so that those with IQs of 120 (and above) are full members of the smart set, those with IQs of 110 are .8 members, and so on. Note that this allows easy quantification of verbal hedges such as "very." "Very smart" might be defined by shifting membership values one position to the right, so that an IQ of 120 entitles one to only .8 membership in the set of very smart people. Fuzzy sets also allow us independently to quantify "dumb" by defining a separate membership function. Fuzzy reasoning makes use of the imprecise information in natural language rules, providing a rigorous mechanism for propagating this uncertainty through the inference process. Further treatment of fuzzy inferencing is beyond this basic primer, but interested readers will find Grzymala-Busse (1991) and McNeill and Thro (1994) helpful.

There are many general introductions to expert systems, including Carrico, Girard, and Jones (1989), Kandel (1992), and Pedersen (1989). Social science work is reviewed in Benfer, Brent, and Furbee (1991), Duffy and Tucker (1995), Garson (1990), Guillet (1989), and Schrodt (in press).

An Extended Example: Taber (1992)

Like the work of Bendor and Moe (1985), the Policy Arguer project (Taber, 1992; Taber & Timpone, 1994b) emerged out of dissatisfaction with current explanations of an important political process—in this case, foreign policy decision making. Most research in this area falls in the lower right quadrant of Figure 1.1, with an emphasis on descriptive realism and microbehavior. Broad theoretical frameworks exist with little systematic quantitative examination, either empirical or theoretical. Some formal models have been developed that generate interesting predictions—for example, game theoretic models of international bargaining or deterrence—but by and large, formal work in the area has seemed too sterile to be compelling to most analysts of foreign policy. These scholars have taken the qualitative path when confronted with the difficult choice between analytically precise, descriptively inaccurate (usually mathematical) models and analytically unfocused, descriptively rich (usually verbal) case studies. An impressive base of qualitative historical case studies exists that provides intimate detail on foreign-policy decision making. Since George and Smoke's (1974) classic book on deterrence, many of these have been embedded in a comparative framework, allowing generalization across cases.

Our frustration with this research area grew from the disjunction, so common in the social sciences, between the complexity of historical processes and theoretical structures on one hand and the simplicity of formal representations of those processes on the other. To reiterate our earlier point, process validity suffers when Occam's razor shaves away important features of the **phenomenal system** along with the irrelevancies. The Policy Arguer (POLI) project is our effort to find a rigorous formal language for expressing the complex theory and case data of foreign-policy analysis (see also Sylvan, Goel, & Chandrasekaran, 1990).

POLI uses expert system methods to model multiple, competing belief systems and their impact on U.S. policy toward Asia. Based on a general theory of foreign-policy decision making first articulated by Snyder, Bruck, and Sapin (1962), it is designed to "re-create" the arguments, both real and for hypothetical situations, that culminate in U.S. policy. Briefly, Snyder, Bruck, and Sapin suggested that national behavior is related to the subjective perceptions and beliefs of national decision makers. Although this may not be controversial, the complexity of any model of this process —for example, operational codes (George, 1969) or cognitive maps (Axelrod, 1976)—seemed insurmountable to most formal modelers. As we have seen, however, expert system methods were designed precisely for this type of problem.

To build POLI, we had to extract the relevant knowledge from an empirical source, express this knowledge formally in POLI's knowledge base, and design an inference engine. Although one theoretically could build a general expert system of foreign-policy decision making, practical considerations recommended a more limited domain: POLI represents U.S. beliefs and debates on policy toward Asia in the 1950s. Moreover, it does not focus on the beliefs of particular individuals. Unlike Michael Young (1994), who models the beliefs of a particular U.S. leader—President Jimmy Carter—we model three broad conceptions of the world, or paradigms, that generally structured U.S. foreign-policy debate in this period. These are militant anticommunism (MAC), pragmatic anticommunism (PAC), and isolationism (ISO).

Militant anticommunists see the world in black and white terms, divided in conflict between the West, defended by the United States, with a monolithic communist movement led by the Soviet Union. The United States must contain communism wherever it threatens. Pragmatic anticommunists, by contrast, see the world in many shades of gray, believing that social, economic, and political instabilities throughout the world make countries vulnerable. Although force may be a last option in protecting the new nations of Asia, PACs believe that social and economic aid will be more effective in advancing U.S. interests. Finally, isolationists argue that the United States must withdraw as much as possible from the dangerous and dirty games of international politics (Taber & Timpone, 1994b). These are the core beliefs of the paradigms, as drawn from the foreign policy literature. What empirical sources exist that detail these paradigms "in action"?

Knowledge engineering most often involves lengthy interviews with the domain experts, but the foreign-policy leaders of the 1950s are unavailable. POLI therefore must rely on documentary sources and content analysis (for a "purely" inductive alternative, see our discussion of ID3 in the next chapter). Because of its availability across the time span, richness of debate, and breadth of coverage, we chose as our source the daily transcript of speeches and debates before Congress found in the *Congressional Record*. Next, we designed a type of content analysis for extracting the "logic" used in discourse (for detail, see Taber & Timpone, 1994b) and applied it to all entries found under the headings "Asia" and "the Far East" in the *Congressional Record* index for the years 1949-1963 (we have expanded this analysis toward the present, though results have not yet been published). This yielded a codesheet, or "propositional inventory," for each entry. The codesheets were sorted according to the three-paradigm typology and into four time periods (1949-1952, 1953-1956, 1957-1960, and 1961-1963).

The second phase of this project involved expressing the "logic of action" in these propositional inventories as structures in 12 knowledge bases, one for each paradigm for each period. The codesheets already separate declarative knowledge—of concepts and conceptual relations—from procedural knowledge—of processes. This division was preserved in the knowledge bases. For each knowledge base, declarative knowledge was expressed in a frame system (Figure 3.4), and procedural knowledge was expressed in a list of IF-THEN rules. An example of a rule representing part of the procedural knowledge of MAC's domino theory is

50

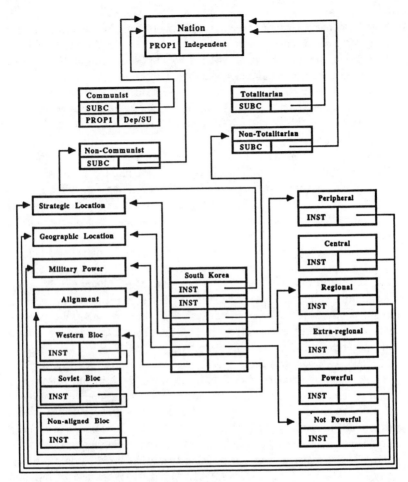

Figure 3.4. A Knowledge Frame From POLI

IF	political system of actor is communist
AND	political system of target is noncommunist
AND	actor and target are contiguous
AND	actor physically threatens target
THEN	target is in danger of falling communist (CF = .9)

Note the certainty factor. Each element of belief in the knowledge bases, either declarative or procedural, has an associated CF, which was calculated as the simple proportion of speeches in the paradigm and period that expressed the belief in the rule or frame entry. Thus, 90% of the speeches by militant anticommunists about Asia for the specific time period invoked the domino theory. Finally, each paradigm, represented as a knowledge base for a given period, has a CF indexing its prevalence in the overall policy system. Isolationism was the paradigm behind 12.5% of speeches from the 1949-1952 period, giving it a CF = .125.

The third major task was designing an inference engine that could operate on the frame systems and rules in the knowledge bases to make inferences about input conditions. (As we have mentioned, division of tasks and phases in an expert system project cannot really be this neat, because prototypes of the knowledge bases must be tested using the inference engine.) For POLI, input consists of an "event" in the form (actor) (verb) (target) (context), where actors, targets, and verbs are concepts that must be defined in the frame systems for POLI to respond, and context includes the date of the event, a CF for degree of confidence that the event actually happened, and any other relevant information. Values for each of these inputs are elicited by POLI's user interface (which we will not describe here).

The inference engine must apply frame-based declarative knowledge to interpret events such as (north korea) (attacks) (south korea) (1950) (CF = .9). The declarative knowledge in Figure 3.4, representing MAC beliefs about South Korea in this period, assigns a range of attributes to the target in the 1950 North Korean attack. For example, South Korea is understood to be a strategically peripheral, geographically regional, weak, West-aligned, noncommunist, nontotalitarian nation (this is only part of MAC's full frame representation for South Korea and does not include the associated CFs). North Korea also is assigned attributes that define it, and the verb "attack" is mapped onto the action "physically threaten."

Once the event is interpreted (POLI can operate on partial interpretations), the inference engine must apply rule-based knowledge to infer a policy recommendation for the U.S. response. POLI uses fuzzy forward reasoning to grow inference chains for each input. Because we were interested in all possible policy arguments given the three paradigms, POLI follows an extreme breadth-first control strategy, in which all rules that match information in working memory fire each cycle, though the same rule cannot be used twice in the same inference chain. POLI continues cycling until one full pass through the rule base fires no rules. It then moves on to the next paradigm's knowledge base, generating a new interpretation of the original input from this paradigm's frame system and a new set of inference chains. The full set of policy recommendations and the lines of reasoning that led to them are interpreted as the policy debate over the U.S. response to the input event.

As we have said, POLI's reasoning is fuzzy in the technical sense that it treats CFs as fuzzy numbers. Although the derivation is beyond the scope of this monograph (Taber, 1991), we can illustrate the simple rules of fuzzy inferencing as applied to the type of uncertainty represented in POLI's knowledge bases. Consider the rule IF {A and B} or {C} THEN {D} with CF = .3. When the premise is certainly true, the conclusion (D) will be believed at the .3 level. The premise often is uncertain and may contain several elements with independent truth values. In this case, two simple computations must be made to assign a CF to the new inference: We must calculate a "global" truth value for the premise, and we must calculate a truth value for the inferred conclusion. POLI computes the premise truth value following the rules for fuzzy sets already described: A global CF is the minimum value of disjunctive elements and the maximum value of conjunctive elements. If working memory for our example contains the "facts" A (CF = .1), B (CF = .9), and C (CF = .2), the global CF for the premise will be max(min(.1, .9), .2) = .2. POLI computes the inference truth value, using the compositional rule of inference, as the minimum of the premise-CF and rule-CF, or min(.2, .3) = .2. D is inferred and added to working memory with CF = .2. This procedure remains faithful to fuzzy set theory, unlike the popular "CF method" (described above), which follows fuzzy procedures to compute the premise truth value but then uses a conditional probability procedure to compute a truth value for the inference.

POLI was tested on both outcome and process levels (for sensitivity tests, see Taber, 1992). First, using an independently compiled record of Asian events and U.S. responses, POLI's strongest recommendations were compared with the actual U.S. responses, finding 138 correct predictions for the 161 events (86%). In a second, more stringent test, removing all possibility that POLI's knowledge bases contained logic coded from Congressional debates about the events being tested, POLI still accurately predicted 75% of the events. Moreover, POLI's performance compares favorably with that of four alternative models from the foreign policy literature. It outdoes the best models available—those based on inertia and organizational process—both in a statistical sense and in terms of theoretical power (i.e., POLI takes raw events as input and produces specific policy recommendations as output, which none of its competitors can do).

POLI's process validity was checked using a multilevel method (see Chapter 5). The overall inference process can be examined as a progression of inference steps, each of which is one link in the chain to a policy recommendation. We can interpret each chain as a line of reasoning and compare it to the actual policy debate for the specific case. POLI's interpretations and lines of reasoning were compared with detailed historical studies of the test cases—the Korean War, Japan's 1953 dispute with South Korea, and the 1958 Taiwan Strait crisis. A full discussion of these comparisons is available elsewhere (Taber, 1991, 1992; Taber & Timpone, 1994b) and will not be reviewed here. It suffices to say that the reasoning of POLI's three paradigms comes very close to the historical debate in each case.

Now that it has been validated and updated, POLI is ready for experimentation, using real and counterfactual situations. One brief counterfactual example should convey the flavor of this analysis. Recall that, in contrast with militant anticommunism's black and white view of the world, the more pragmatic view asserted that most of the attraction of communism or totalitarianism stemmed from the social and economic instabilities within former colonies. In 1965, when the major escalations of U.S. involvement in Vietnam occurred, militant anticommunism dominated. Our first simple counterfactual question was "What might have happened had pragmatists dominated?" Table 3.1 contrasts the top 10 policy recommendations of the real, MAC-dominated system with those of the hypothetical PAC-dominated system. They clearly are very different: PAC's are more concerned about the effect of U.S. action on emerging former colonies. That outcomes would have been different is easily predicted without POLI. More interesting is that POLI offers a process explanation for the difference, locating the specific "logical linkages" that take these two paradigms in different directions. In this case, as earlier in Korea, the key difference is the centrality of the strongest version of the domino theory to MAC thinkers. PAC is concerned about a subtler, nonmilitary form of falling dominoes and makes its recommendations accordingly. This is the key divergence in the lines of argument.

Hybrid Systems

Many of the knowledge-based systems that have been developed combine several representation languages. For example, POLI uses a frame system to represent declarative knowledge and a rule base for procedural knowledge. John Anderson's ACT* model of human cognition (1983) uses a combination of semantic networks, frames, and rules. In modeling

TABLE 3.1
Counterfactual Example: Vietnam

MAC-dominated (MAC CF = .9, PAC CF = .1)
  communicate commitment to protect target
  advocate collective security agreement in region
  withdraw or refuse diplomatic recognition of actor
  pressure allies to sanction actor
  lodge protest in united nations
  increase military support to regional noncommunists
  increase material support to regional noncommunists
  communicate the containment line in asia
  increase military aid to target
  support suppression of revolutionary movement in target

PAC-dominated (MAC CF = .1, PAC CF = .9)
  raise problem in united nations security council
  verbally support target, but reduce defense commitment
  advocate collective security agreement in region
  increase financial assistance in region
  increase development assistance in region
  publicly repudiate colonialism
  avoid direct u.s. military involvement in asia
  consult with asian leaders before taking action
  promote principles of majority rule, freedom, and equality
  allow independent foreign policy for asian allies

---

real-world systems and complex theories, hybrid representations may facilitate faithful translation of processes and structures into a computer model. One can force a representation language to express almost any kind of knowledge (e.g., production rules could be represented in a semantic network by defining an "implies" link that would directionally connect antecedent and consequent conditions), but such representations may become clumsy and unnatural. We advise careful consideration of the nature of the knowledge to be represented when choosing formal languages.

4. MODELS OF MACHINE LEARNING

For two reasons, one theoretical and one practical, computational learning methods are important to social scientists. First, most social systems are adaptive. Good theoretical models of these systems ultimately may have to grapple with learning or evolutionary adaptation. Second, machine-learning methods can be used for knowledge acquisition, which is generally the most time-consuming part of a computational project. For example, one might use machine-learning methods to induce the rules for an expert system directly from empirical data. This chapter provides brief descriptions of three methods with impressive pedigrees in computer science that are finding wider use today in the social sciences.

Connectionist models are a class of artificial intelligence with roots extending back to the work of Donald Hebb in the 1940s. Unlike the AI methods discussed in the last chapter, however, **connectionism** (also called parallel distributed processing) does not subscribe to the knowledge representation hypothesis, at least not in its explicitly symbolic sense (Reichgelt, 1991). Conventional knowledge models assume that knowledge is stored in the mind (and hence in the models) as structures of symbols, with each symbol having some independent meaning. In rough analogy to the brain, however, the artificial **neural networks** of connectionism represent knowledge as configurations of activation states distributed throughout the network (Rumelhart & McClelland, 1989). These should not be confused with semantic networks, in which each node has independent semantic content.

ID3 (Quinlan, 1979, 1986) is the best-known method for inducing classification rules from a set of examples. This sort of inductive analysis is intrinsically useful, but the greatest contribution of ID3 and its descendants may be in overcoming the "knowledge acquisition bottleneck." Traditional knowledge engineering for expert systems (as described in the last chapter) is both costly and limited to what human experts can articulate. Rule induction methods allow researchers to extract domain knowledge directly from examples, represented in a standard rectangular data set.

Genetic algorithms, inspired by the operation of chromosomes in carrying and modifying evolutionary information, were developed by John Holland (1975). They are useful for studying evolutionary processes at the system level, where micro behavior has macro effects, and as an alternative method for statistical optimization.

Connectionist Models

Neural networks consist of a large number of densely linked processing units. Each unit is quite simple, usually storing a single numeric value called its activation. Each unit is connected to many other units in the net (sometimes to all other units), and its activation may be communicated across these links. We call the transmissions from a unit "output values" and those to a unit "input values." Values can be transmitted unaltered, but neural networks with slightly more complex units may modify the value according to a simple mathematical function. For example, a threshold function may allow a unit to pass its activation value when activation exceeds some parameter. Connections, which are usually unidirectional, are assigned weights. Positive weights excite, while negative weights inhibit, the linked unit. In computing the net input for a unit, a process called **propagation**, all input values are multiplied by the weights of the corresponding links, and these products are summed. The net input to a unit is then modified by a simple mathematical function, producing a new activation value for the unit. Because the functions that may transform activation values on input and output from a unit remain the same through the life of a network, the knowledge that a network is "trained" to represent lies in its overall configuration of connection weights. How effectively a network can store knowledge, however, depends also on the nature of these functions and the "shape" of the network.

Neural networks may be connected in many ways, but rather than delving too deeply, we will describe one common type, **layered feedforward systems**. Such networks define different types of processing units, configured in layers, and feed activation through the layers in one direction. Figure 4.1 illustrates such a network, in which there is a layer of input units, two layers of hidden units, and a layer of output units. Consider the simple example in Figure 4.2 with the following network definition: (a) units have activation values of 0 or 1; (b) the output of each unit is its activation value; (c) the net input to each unit is the sum of the inputs from all connected units multiplied by their connection weights; and (d) a threshold function defines the propagation of activation, such that a unit's activation becomes 1 when net input is equal to or greater than 5, and is otherwise 0. Input and output are observed as activation patterns of 0s and 1s. If input is [0, 1, 1], net input for unit i is $(0 \times 7) + (1 \times 5) + (1 \times -2) = 3$. Because this is less than the threshold of 5, i's activation is 0. Following this procedure for a variety of input patterns, we obtain the output patterns in Table 4.1. Knowledge is stored in the connection weights in the sense that the input

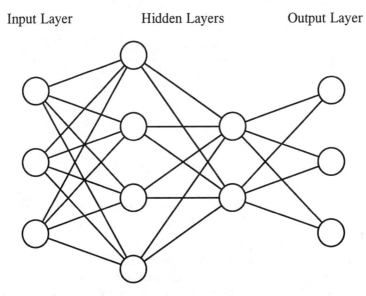

Figure 4.1. A Simple Feedforward Neural Network

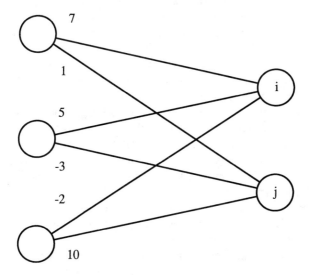

Figure 4.2. A Neural Network Example

TABLE 4.1

A Neural Network Example

Input	Net Input (i, j)	Output
0 0 0	0, 0	0 0
0 0 1	–2, 10	0 1
0 1 0	5, –3	1 0
0 1 1	3, 7	0 1
1 0 0	7, 1	1 0
1 0 1	5, 11	1 1
1 1 0	12, –2	1 0
1 1 1	10, 8	1 1

patterns can have meaning (i.e., they symbolize something) and they are transformed into output patterns that also can have meaning. An input pattern might symbolize, for example, a sequence of international events, and in a properly trained network, the output pattern might symbolize predicted responses to those events (Schrodt, in press).

Layered feedforward networks pass activation from the input layer, through each hidden layer one at a time, and then to the output layer. The more hidden layers there are, the more cycles of computation are needed to assign activation values (e.g., one hidden layer means we need one cycle to pass values to the hidden layer and another to pass values to the output layer). As a general rule, more complex models with more layers can store more knowledge (i.e., at least one hidden unit per independent feature or dimension of the problem is required). Training connectionist models therefore can be very taxing computationally. Notice, however, that processing is parallel within each cycle. (**Parallel processing** means that procedures and computations are done simultaneously; **serial processing** means they are done in sequence.) Parallel processing hardware—both parallel computers and neural network chips embedded in otherwise serial devices—can alleviate some of the computational demand. Because of the expense of special hardware, most researchers still simulate parallel processes on serial processing computers.

The great advantage of connectionist models, their proponents claim, is their ability to "learn automatically" through a very simple process of changing the connection weights according to some learning rule. A model thus can be trained to output a prediction for the probability of war whenever particular streams of international events are symbolically indicated by the input pattern. Although various learning rules have been proposed for connectionist models, we restrict our discussion to the best known, the **delta rule.** The delta rule might be called a "tuning rule" in that it is designed to change connection weights incrementally toward their "correct" values. Reichgelt (1991, pp. 197-204) presents a good description of the delta rule in the context of Rumelhart and McClelland's models (1989); a simpler description of what has become known as the generalized delta rule is more appropriate here.

Training a network proceeds in two stages. First, we present an input pattern and an output pattern that we want the network to associate. The network produces its own output pattern on the basis of the hidden layers and connection weights between the input and output layers. The network then compares its output with the desired output, calculating for each unit an error signal. This error signal is calculated recursively, starting with the output units, whose error signals are simply the difference between their activation value and the target for their activation. This error signal "propagates backward" to hidden layers, so that each receives an error signal, computed as the sum of the products of all error signals passed backward from the output layer (or previous hidden layer) multiplied by their connection weights. Once all units have an error signal, the connection weights among the units are revised according to the formula

$$\Delta w_{ij} = \eta \delta_{pi} a_{pj} \qquad (4.1)$$

where Δw_{ij} is the change in the weight linking units i and j, δ_{pi} is the error signal to unit i given input pattern p, a_{pj} is the activation value of unit j given input pattern p, and η is a parameter controlling rate of learning. This rule modifies weights so they should move closer to values that will generate the desired output from the given input. In training a neural network, one generally presents the training cases repeatedly, until the weights converge on appropriate values.

Connectionist models are now commonly used for many forecasting problems, for which the task is to match appropriate output patterns (predictions) with an input pattern symbolizing current conditions. For example, Blum (1992) developed a simple stock market predictor model. This neural net predicts the changes in price of selected stocks on the basis of previous price fluctuations, volume and volatility for selected stocks, interest and exchange rates, standard stock averages (e.g., the Dow Jones Industrial Average), and direct performance indicators from the New York Stock Exchange (NYSE). Altogether, 106 inputs were selected (on the basis of intuition and statistical analysis of existing data), including 90 individual "bellwether" issues and 16 general macroeconomic indicators. The model takes these 106 inputs for the three preceding weeks, so there are 318 input units. All input and activation values are normalized to range between 0 and 1. Each of the 30 stocks to be predicted is represented by one output unit. Blum designed the model as a layered feedforward network using back propagation methods to adjust connection weights, just as in our examples above. Unfortunately, there is no direct way to discern how many independent features exist in this forecasting problem, short of running an exploratory factor analysis on the data. Blum knew, however, that there would be fewer dimensions than inputs and more than outputs, so he chose to implement 64 hidden units. If this proved not to be adequate, the network would be unable to learn, at which time he could increase the number of hidden units.

Once the network was defined and programmed, Blum trained it on historical data matching real 3-week inputs with real 4-week outputs. Eventually, the model perfectly "postdicted" all the training data. Although he does not take his application this far, Blum recommends that the model be tested against other historical data before using it to guide any real stock market decisions.

Further discussion of connectionist models can be found in Adeli and Hung (1995), Khanna (1990), Reichgelt (1991), Rumelhart and McClelland (1989), and Schalkoff (1992). Garson (1991) and Schrodt (1991b) provide social science examples.

ID3

A classic problem from machine learning involves discovering a decision tree sufficient for classifying a set of empirical examples. Consider the hypothetical data in Table 4.2 concerning enrollments at ten high schools. To explain the variation in enrollments, we might try to discover a set of classification rules that would cover all the schools in the sample. A human expert in school choice, for example, might tell us that "IF crime is low or moderate, and test scores are average or above, THEN school enrollments should increase." Figure 4.3 represents this classification information as a simple decision tree, in which crime is the root, test scores are lower branches, and enrollment forms the leaves. If we were building a knowledge-based model to predict school enrollments, we might consult such experts. What if we do not have access to experts, or what if we

TABLE 4.2
Hypothetical Data on School Enrollments

School	Enrollment	Facilities	Teacher Experience	Crime	Test Scores	Class Size
1	up	good	high	moderate	above average	large
2	down	poor	low	moderate	average	large
3	up	excellent	high	low	above average	small
4	up	good	low	low	above average	large
5	down	good	low	high	above average	large
6	down	poor	low	high	average	large
7	up	good	high	low	above average	small
8	up	excellent	low	low	average	large
9	down	good	low	moderate	below average	large
10	down	good	low	high	average	large

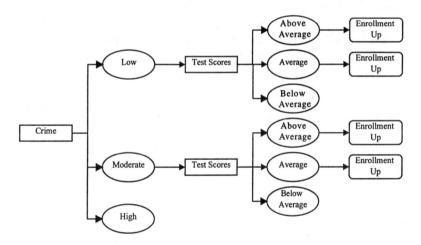

Figure 4.3. An Example Decision Tree

question the ability of experts to articulate their knowledge? Rather than the traditional knowledge engineering approach described in the last chapter, we might look to data on school choice and enrollments (presumably a much larger set of variables and cases than Table 4.2). ID3 is a general algorithm that can induce classification rules directly from data. As Schrodt (in press, p. 5.4) puts it, ID3 "is the linear regression of machine learning methods."

62

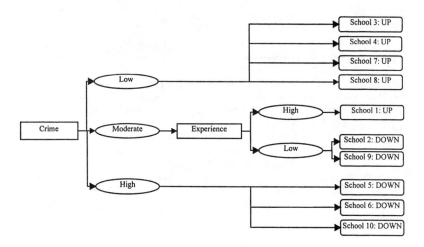

Figure 4.4. A Classification Tree for School Enrollments

ID3 is based on a method for building classification trees from nominal data called the Concept Learning System (CLS). First developed by Earl Hunt (Hunt, Marin, & Stone, 1966), CLS grows classification trees from a root node, through branch nodes, to leaf nodes, successively refining the tree until all examples in the data can be classified unambiguously. Figure 4.4 depicts a classification tree for the data in Table 4.2, illustrating a set of decision rules that will be discussed below. Which concept should form the root and which the branches? We might have rooted a tree on test scores or class size, for example. In fact, no unique decision tree exists to classify data like that in Table 4.2. Quinlan's (1979, 1986) innovation in designing ID3 was to grow trees from root to leaves in order of the discriminating power of the features of the data. ID3 chooses for the root node the data feature that "does the most work" in classifying the examples, for the lower branches the most discriminating features that remain, and so on, using algorithms based on the reduction of **entropy**. (Note the parallels to principal components analysis.)

Formally, if there are N values of the dependent variable (e.g., "enrollment" in Table 4.2), $c_1, c_2, \ldots, c_N$, and the proportion of data cases with a given value i is $p(c_i)$, then the total entropy of the dependent variable C is

$$H(C) = -\sum_{i=1}^{N} p(c_i)\log_2 p(c_i) \qquad (4.2)$$

If we apply this formula to Table 4.2, we find the cases split equally between the two values of enrollment ("up" and "down"), yielding an entropy of $-[5/10 \log_2(5/10) + 5/10 \log_2(5/10)] = 1.00$.

What we really need to know, however, is the most efficient order in which to build the classification tree. In terms of information theory, which feature should we branch on in order to minimize entropy in the dependent variable (i.e., maximize information gain)? For this, we must calculate the conditional entropy of each possible classification at the current node of the decision tree. In our example, we must first find out which feature of schools minimizes entropy in school enrollments and make it the root of the tree. Then we must examine each subtree from the root and find the remaining features that minimize entropy, and so on. ID3 employs the same simple algorithm recursively at each possible branch of the tree. Given a feature A with M values $a_1, a_2, \ldots, a_M$, the information gained by looking only at examples for which $A = a_j$ is

$$H(C|a_j) = -\sum_{i=1}^{N} p(c_i|a_j)\log_2 p(c_i|a_j) \qquad (4.3)$$

For example, the entropy of classifying schools by their enrollment is reduced to zero if we look only at the four cases in which crime is low (in all four cases enrollment is up). The entropy of the classification information in the feature "crime" is the sum of the entropies for each value of crime ($H(C|\text{crime}) = H(C|\text{crime} = \text{low}) + H(C|\text{crime} = \text{moderate}) + H(C|\text{crime} = \text{high})$). More generally, the entropy for classifying examples given the information in some feature A as defined above is

$$H(C|A) = \sum_{j=1}^{M} p(a_j)H(A|a_j) \qquad (4.4)$$

Calculating this for each of the five features in Table 4.2, we find that entropy is minimized when we make crime the root of the classification tree. When crime is low, enrollments are up; when crime is high, enrollments are down. There is no remaining variance in the dependent variable at these nodes, so no further classification is necessary. There is still variance in enrollments when crime is moderate, however, so we must find another feature and add a branch to the tree off the crime = moderate branch. We do so in exactly the way we chose the root, considering the entropy reduction offered by all four remaining features and choosing to branch on that feature that minimizes remaining entropy. For our data, "teacher experience" perfectly classifies the cases of moderate crime. At this point, all the examples in our "training set" are classified—they form the leaves in the decision tree pictured in Figure 4.4. Translating this into classification rules, we find that (a) IF crime = low THEN enrollment = up, (b) IF crime = high THEN enrollment = down, (c) IF crime = moderate AND teacher experience = high THEN enrollment is up, and (d) IF crime = moderate AND teacher experience = low THEN enrollment is down.

The ID3 algorithm is relatively simple, but used recursively, it may become taxing computationally. When the data set is too large for the above procedure to be practical, ID3 can use an "experiment-planning approach," in which a subset is selected (usually randomly) from the training cases for ID3 processing (Cohen & Feigenbaum, 1982; Quinlan, 1979). Once a classification tree has been constructed for this subset, the rest of the cases in the data set are searched for exceptions to the classification rules in the tree. A new subset is formed that combines some of these exceptions with some of the cases from the prior subset, and the ID3 algorithm is run again to create a new classification tree. This process continues until no exceptions remain in the full data set.

Good general descriptions of ID3 can be found in Quinlan (1979, 1986), Cohen and Feigenbaum (1982), Thompson and Thompson (1986), and Schrodt (in press). Schrodt also provides a nice social science application. Finally, several important extensions of the approach described here are reported in Unseld and Mallery (1993) and in the four *Machine Learning* volumes (Kodratoff & Michalski, 1990; Michalski, Carbonell, & Mitchell, 1983, 1986; Michalski & Tecuci, 1994).

Genetic Algorithms

Genetic algorithms may best be introduced through the metaphor of natural evolution (Davis & Steenstrup, 1987). The problem each species faces in a complex natural environment is the search for advantageous adaptations. The information accumulated by each species through its evolutionary history is contained in its members' chromosomes and passed on when parents reproduce. Evolution offers a solution to the basic problem faced by species by modifying the chromosomal makeup of offspring according to mutation, inversion of chromosomal information, and cross-over of chromosomal information. Random mutation can introduce beneficial adaptations (though it is more likely to introduce nonadaptive solutions) through chance modifications of genetic material, inversion allows individual genes (bits of genetic information) to move on chromosomes so that beneficial genes can cluster, and crossover exchanges corresponding clusters of genes between the two parents' chromosomes. Crossover is particularly useful in that it greatly increases the chance of beneficial adaptation by allowing the positive changes stored in the chromosomes of both parents to affect the chromosomes of offspring. Using these mechanisms, evolution "searches for solutions" in parallel, combining "better" features and eventually approaching "best" features.

Genetic algorithms likewise search a problem space for solutions, storing potential solutions in a simple form, and modifying stored solutions according to mutation, inversion, and crossover. They can be used to model evolutionary processes, as in the extended example of the evolution of cooperative strategies, or to solve complex optimization problems (e.g., as an alternative to maximum likelihood estimation). Genetic algorithms are particularly useful because they often converge on a solution more rapidly than do other methods, and they can overcome the problem of local maxima, finding global solutions for cases in which other methods fail. They are a tool for both formal and empirical modeling.

Genetic algorithm models have four components: (a) **chromosomes**, which store potential solutions to a problem as sequences of information bits; (b) an **initial population** of imperfect solutions; (c) an **evaluation function** that rates the quality of solutions (as natural selection rates the quality of adaptive changes); and (d) **genetic algorithms**, which modify the chromosomes of offspring during reproduction. A great deal of research has been done that can guide the choices modelers must make for each of these components. Most research represents chromosomes as **bit strings**, in which each bit stores one binary piece of information (0 or 1). Solution populations may be initialized randomly, or a modeler may use knowledge of the problem to generate "best guesses." Evaluation functions may search aggressively for optimal solutions or use gentler heuristics. Several variations of the three basic genetic operators are used. For example, crossover may divide chromosomes in half, fitting one parent's first half with the second's second half, or it may pull sequences from the middle of one chromosome to exchange with sequences from the other.

As we have mentioned, genetic algorithms can be used to solve difficult optimization problems. Consider the problem represented in Figure 4.5, depicting the decision spaces of two people on gun control and health care. The first person likes moderate positions on both issues and has a single-

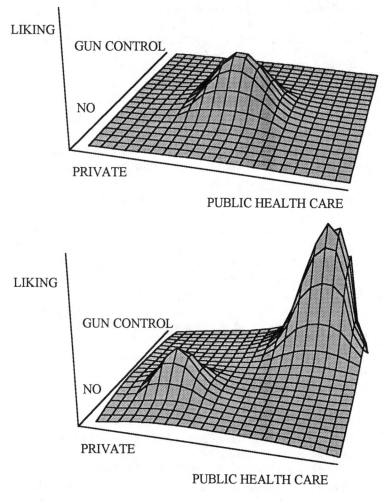

Figure 4.5. Hypothetical Policy Preferences

peaked preference function. The second person prefers tough gun control
and public health care but likes no government intervention on both issues
better than middle-of-the-road positions, yielding a multipeaked preference function. Standard calculus-based hill-climbing methods will find the
global maximum easily in the first case. (Hill climbing refers to a search
method that always moves upward on the path of steepest ascent from

wherever it starts until it can climb no farther.) Hill climbing may become trapped in the local maximum in the latter case, failing to find this person's most liked position. A genetic algorithm search can find global maxima even for multipeaked functions, by preserving incremental improvements through inversion and crossover and trying new solutions through mutation. The combination of favoring both improvement and novel solutions allows genetic algorithms to escape from local maxima. Generalization of this technique is very useful for many formal modeling problems; for example, classifier systems have become popular for modeling many learning systems. Genetic algorithms are also increasingly used in place of standard maximum likelihood estimators for empirical analysis.

Adeli and Hung (1995), Davis and Steenstrup (1987), Goldberg (1989), and Rawlins (1991) present lucid introductions and review the literature. An application of these ideas to bureaucratic learning can be found in Schrodt (in press).

An Extended Example: Axelrod (1987)

Robert Axelrod has long been interested in the evolution of cooperation among individual self-interested actors (Axelrod, 1984, 1987). In particular, he seeks explanations for the emergence of cooperation in environments that contain strong incentives not to cooperate (e.g., "live-and-let-live" systems that apparently emerged for some troops facing each other across entrenched battle lines in World War I), because those who do cooperate should slowly disappear under the pressures of natural selection. To formally express this type of situation, Axelrod chose a version of the "iterated prisoner's dilemma" (IPD) from game theory.

> In the Prisoner's Dilemma, two individuals can either cooperate [C] or defect [D]. The payoff to a player affects its reproductive success. No matter what the other does, the selfish choice of defection yields a higher payoff than cooperation. But if both defect, both do worse than if both cooperated (Axelrod, 1987, p. 32).

Table 4.3 depicts the classic payoff matrix for this game. The iterated version of the prisoner's dilemma simply allows the same two individuals to meet several times, so that they may consider a future of interactions. A strategy can be defined generally as an individual's "decision rule which specifies the probability of cooperation or defection as a function of the history of interaction so far" (Axelrod, 1987, p. 32). In this research,

68

TABLE 4.3
Prisoner's Dilemma Payoff Matrix

Row Player	Column Player	
	Cooperate	*Defect*
Cooperate	(3, 3) Reward for Mutual Cooperation	(0, 5) Row: Sucker's Payoff Column: Temptation to Defect
Defect	(5, 0) Row: Temptation to Defect Column: Sucker's Payoff	(1, 1) Punishment for Mutual Defection

NOTE: Payoffs are listed row first (Row, Column).

Axelrod focuses on strategies that key the participants' choices (C or D) deterministically on the outcomes of their last three interactions (there are four outcomes each play, so there are 4 × 4 × 4 = 64 possible histories of the last three plays). One such strategy, for example, tries to take advantage of the opponent by defecting whenever two of the three prior plays ended in mutual cooperation. Axelrod is interested in finding out which strategies survive in an evolutionary environment composed of a set of individual actors, each behaving according to one of the possible strategies.

To explore this research problem, Axelrod used the genetic algorithm method, which was described with four components: (a) chromosomes that contain possible solutions to the survival problem encoded as strings of information bits (genes), (b) an initial population of strategies, (c) an evaluation function for deciding what strategies survive and reproduce, and (d) genetic algorithms, which define the permissible operations for modifying chromosomes during reproduction. Once these four components are specified, the model can be run on a computer to determine which solutions will emerge within the competitive environment. In this example, the chromosomes encoded possible strategies for the IPD game as strings of 70 bits, with 64 of these bits telling the actor carrying the chromosome what to do in response to each of the 64 possible histories of the last three plays (for example, if the 52nd bit represents the situation "mutual-C, mutual-C, sucker's payoff" and holds a D, the actor will defect when this historical pattern occurs) and 6 genes specifying what to do when there is no history of interaction. Second, Axelrod randomly generated his initial population of strategies. Third, the effectiveness of an actor was calculated as its average score up to the current moment, as defined by the payoff matrix in Table 4.3. Because relatively successful pairs of individuals reproduce (generating two offspring), effectiveness determined survival rates. Fourth, two genetic algorithms were used: mutation randomly altered a small proportion of the 70 genes, and crossover was applied. Axelrod used a form of crossover that cut random points in the parents' chromosomes, splicing the head of each chromosome to the tail of the other. For example (Axelrod, 1987, p. 35), consider two parents, one that always cooperates (whose chromosome is a string of 70 Cs) and one that always defects (a string of 70 Ds). Crossover might cut the two parent chromosomes between the fifth and sixth genes, so that one child has five Cs followed by 65 Ds and the other has 5 Ds followed by 65 Cs.

Axelrod's simulations ran 50 generations of 20 individuals each. Between generational changes, the individuals in a generation interacted as follows: Each of the 20 actors met 8 others, chosen randomly, for an iterated game, where each game lasted for 151 moves. Each actor therefore made 1208 moves per generation. The average score for each actor was computed, and the highest scoring actors were paired randomly for reproduction, during which mutation and crossover occurred for a set proportion of chromosomes (one crossover and one half mutation per chromosome). The two offspring from each set of parents formed the new generation.

In Axelrod's words,

> The results were quite remarkable: from a strictly random start, the genetic algorithm evolved populations whose median member was just as successful as the best rule from [Axelrod's earlier] tournament, TIT FOR TAT [TFT]. Most of the strategies that evolved actually resemble TIT FOR TAT. (1987, p. 36)

TFT is a simple strategy that has proved remarkably resilient in computer tournaments of possible strategies for playing the prisoner's dilemma. It always repeats the opponent's last play, starting with an initial play of cooperation. The strategies that evolved in Axelrod's genetic algorithm simulation resembled TFT in that they cooperated after three mutual cooperations, defected when the opponent defected out of the blue (they were "provokable"), returned to cooperation when the opponent did (they were "forgiving"), and no longer forgave after three mutual defections (they "accept a rut"). These strategies, although not identical to TFT, evolved from random beginnings to share most of the characteristics that make TFT such a successful strategy. They demonstrate—using a new, highly inductive method—that forgiving strategies that cooperate with each other unless provoked can develop and succeed in a cutthroat evolutionary environment.

5. EVALUATING COMPUTATIONAL MODELS

The idea of evaluation is central "for improving the artistry of speculations" (Lave & March, 1993, p. 52). As we argued in our introduction, models are integral to the development of theoretical understanding. Because many models (and many types of models) can be imagined to represent a theory, we need procedures for evaluation. Now that we have an overview of computational modeling techniques, the next question is: How can we tell a good computational model from a bad one? Lave and March (1993) offer three standards that may be applied to any scientific model: Truth, Beauty, and Justice. The various criteria of Truth focus on a model's accuracy in portraying the empirical or theoretical system it represents. Beauty considers aesthetic and utilitarian standards. Finally, Justice takes into account the real-world implications of a model, especially those that affect quality of life. In this chapter, we will apply these general standards to the evaluation of computational models (see Figure 5.1).

Truth

The most important hurdle for any scientific statement to cross is Truth, and a variety of methods have been developed for assessing the correctness of a hypothesis. The ephemeral nature of truth makes the search for it more the goal of the social sciences than its actual attainment. Thus, in assessing the accuracy of models, we need to set baselines for comparison. One might, for example, compare a model's performance with chance, with the expectations of "experts," or with the performance of competing models. Moreover, different dimensions of accuracy should be considered, including **outcome validity**, **process validity**, **internal validity**, and **reliability**. Outcome validity is the familiar goal of behavioral science. It measures the degree of correspondence between a model's output (its predictions) and real-world data. Process validity assesses the correspondence between a model's mechanisms and the processes in the real-world system. Internal validity assesses the internal logic of a model—whether it accurately represents the theory or pretheory on which it is based. Reliability examines the robustness of stochastic models.

Process validity is an important goal for many computational modelers, but two qualifications are necessary. First, several of the methods we describe are rarely used with the goal of process validity in mind. For example, despite their rough analogy to biological systems, genetic algorithms may be used as classification or optimization systems with no regard

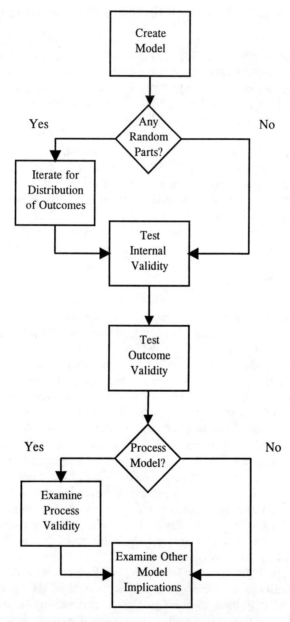

Figure 5.1. General Stages of Computational Model Evaluation

for process validity, and neural networks may more naturally represent organizations than individual brains (Schrodt, in press). Second, like predictive accuracy, process validity is a goal only imperfectly attained in any model. Complete homomorphism (i.e., the model is a perfect symbolization of the theory that perfectly describes real-world processes, so that all three levels are intertranslatable at the logical level) is impossible and undesirable. It makes no more sense to insist on "complete" process validity than to require that 100% of the variance be explained in a regression model.

Note that we will not review specific statistical methods, because they are not unique to computational modeling. Depending on the type of project, a computational model may be tested using correlations, analysis of variance, linear or nonlinear regression, tests for comparison of means, or other methods. A good general familiarity with statistical techniques therefore is as important for a computational modeler as for other social scientists.

Outcome Validity

Almost without exception, the methods for testing the accuracy of hypotheses focus on the degree of correspondence between a model's predictions and real-world behavior, that is, on outcome validity. (Although we will use the term "prediction," the outputs of social science computational models are often actually **postdiction**; that is, their outputs correspond to events that already have occurred.) This remains the first test any model must pass to be useful, and computational models should be no exception. Computational modelers, however, are notoriously disinterested statisticians. One problem is that it is not entirely clear how to test a computational model's predictions. A simple comparison of a model's overall predictions with empirical data may not suffice. Computational models may be so complex, containing so many parameters, variables, and relationships, that one cannot determine which parts of the model are falsified by an inaccurate prediction. Computational modelers are justifiably reluctant to discard the entire model if some predictions fail. There may be insufficient control for a clear test of the overall model. Similarly, no clear standards exist that define acceptable levels of predictive success. When they are tested, computational models often achieve a high percentage of correct predictions; POLI, for example, correctly predicted more than 85% of U.S. responses to Asian events (Taber, 1992). Is this an acceptable level of performance for a model this detailed?

To answer this question, one needs to compare the predictive success of a computational model with other competitive models of the process, perhaps other computational models. POLI's predictive accuracy, for example, compared favorably with that of several models of organizational process. We can use simple statistical tests to find out if the computational model's performance truly is better than that of other models.

Sometimes it is possible to test separately the components of a large computational model, holding other elements constant. For example, the different relationships of many models might be broken apart and tested, for they each make definite predictions. Once the components are individually verified, an interactive model may be tested more clearly. Taken to the extreme, this line of argument suggests that each individual component of a model be separately tested, then tested in interaction (which is not likely to be practical). Rule-based models, for example, may be seen as collections of conditional hypotheses. When we compare such a model's predictions with data, we actually are testing a series of hypotheses from the knowledge base. Consider a knowledge base with 10 rules. Each rule, and each possible chain of rules, is a hypothesis. When the model is given input, all chains that grow culminate in inferences that may be checked against real data. Each successful "test" supports the validity of that particular inference chain but says nothing about the validity of other parts of the rule base. For large rule bases, unfortunately, it is not practical to test each "hypothesis."

As a practical matter, one must be careful to preserve some independent test data when building a computational model. Knowledge-based models, for example, contain a great deal of data extracted from domain experts, from archival documents, or by running a rule generator (e.g., ID3) on quantified data. Similarly, neural networks learn from training data. In some sense, these models are representations of the data used in building them, so they cannot be tested using the same data. To avoid this problem, one might test the model on a separately collected sample of data from the same domain. For example, anthropologist Louanna Furbee's model of the soil classification expertise of Peruvian farmers (1989) was built on interviews of a sample of farmers in the Colca Valley; it was tested (and revised) through consultations with other folk experts. Alternatively, Furbee might have tested the model in similar but slightly different domains (e.g., similar Andean valleys). Taber (1992) divided his data temporally and tested POLI's predictions against data from a subsequent time period. Philip Schrodt (1991b, in press) used a classic split sample design in his neural network analyses, dividing his data into training and test samples. However one does it, a meaningful test must use data that are independent from that used in building the model.

An added complication concerns the potential for undisciplined computational modeling noted in the first chapter. Although flexibility is a strength of these techniques, it creates the potential for abuse as well. Computational models are formal representations of theories about real-world systems, but they are not constrained by observed empirical reality. For example, one could develop highly speculative models of the personalities of historical figures or of cultural evolution based more on conjecture than on observation. These models, though interesting, would be unlikely to add to scientific knowledge unless their plausibility (better yet, their validity) could be assessed.

In our view, the outcome validity of computational models should be tested. At a minimum, their global predictions should be compared directly with real-world data. A computational model that does not produce reasonably accurate overall predictions is unlikely to be a reasonable representation and should be modified or discarded. Better still, a model's success should be compared with that of competing models, and ideally these competitors should be the strongest offered in the field. Given the greater investments of time and resources of a computational model, it is sensible to require it to beat the state of the art. Even here, however, one may prefer a more complex computational model even if it does not lead to a substantial improvement in outcome validity, if it models more accurately than its competitors the processes involved. The most thorough test would be multilevel, examining the predictions of a model's logical components as well as its overall predictions.

Process Validity

We have argued for more emphasis on process validity—the correspondence between a model's mechanisms and the real-world processes that produce the output we normally test. Unfortunately, there is no straightforward way to assess the validity of a theoretical process. In the absence of a direct test, one generally is reduced to arguing for the plausibility of the theorized process. We can suggest three methods for supporting or undermining claims of process validity. First is simple face validity. Do the processes in the model seem reasonable to experts in the field? This approach to face validity is most commonly used for several of the computational methods discussed in previous chapters. Expert systems, for example, are designed explicitly to mimic the decision making of experts, so a natural first (unfortunately, often the last) test is to ask the experts what they think of the model's performance. A slightly more stringent form of face validation follows an extension of the famous **Turing test** (Turing, 1950): If a model's performance (process and output) cannot be distinguished from that of the real system by independent human evaluators, the model is considered process valid. **Sensitivity analysis** can be used to facilitate face validation, as will be discussed in greater detail in a later section. For now, we can say that the parameters in a model may be systematically varied to see whether the model behaves as expected. This requires, of course, that one already knows generally how the model should behave under certain conditions (obviously, one need not know how the model will behave under all conditions).

Second, the validity of the model's assumptions may be tested directly to lend support to the acceptance of a model's processes. If tested, some assumptions would certainly be false, because models are only caricatures of reality. Given an assumption failure, one would have to assess how seriously the inaccuracy affects the model's behavior. Here again, sensitivity analysis would be helpful, because it allows us to find out which parts of a model produce which behavior. The degree to which this false assumption is important to a causal theory affects how much it undermines the process validity of the model.

Third, outcome validation, particularly multilevel testing, may be used to examine process validity. A model's processes may be reduced to subprocesses, which may themselves be reduced to subprocesses, theoretically all the way down to the primitive level. This is one reason that good flowcharts for a computational model are indispensable. Each subprocess makes sub-outcome predictions that possibly can be tested. Although this differs from a true test of processes, it does lend support to the validation of process theories. This promising approach, however, makes ever increasing demands on measurement, which may not be answered in existing empirical techniques or in available data. At some point, decomposing processes into subcomponents is likely to lead to a problem reminiscent of Heisenberg's Uncertainty Principle: The measurement techniques used to evaluate accuracy may actually influence results. Moreover, data measured on an increasingly small scale eventually may be overwhelmed by noise from standard measurement error. Keeping these hazards in mind, however, this method may be the most powerful way of assessing the process plausibility of complex computational models.

A variation on this technique was used in the POLI expert system project (Taber, 1991; Taber & Timpone, 1994b), which represents the reasoning

77

and debates on U.S. foreign policy toward Asia in the 1950s. Each of the policies recommended by the model is generated by a general process composed of routines and subroutines, including an event interpretation subroutine and an inferencing subroutine. Moreover, the inferencing subroutine can be broken into chains of reasoning based on IF-THEN rules from the model's knowledge base. The interpretations and reasoning offered by POLI as outputs from these subroutines were compared to detailed historical case studies of actual U.S. decision making about Asian events. The degree of correspondence between the reasoning in the model and that found in the real-world system strongly supports its process plausibility.

Internal Validity, Reliability, and Sensitivity Analysis

As introduced in Chapter 1, a computational modeling project proceeds through several phases: A theory is developed to account for a real-world phenomenon; a formal model of that theory is developed; a computer representation of that formal model is written; and the model is tested and analyzed. The testing phase is interested in the quality of the implemented theory—how well it accounts for the real-world phenomenon (both process and output). One cannot meaningfully evaluate the theory unless the computer model is a faithful—that is, internally valid—representation of the theory, and the more complex a theory, the greater the danger of significant "slippage" when building and programming the formal model. Consideration of internal validity thus is logically prior to outcome and process validation, but how can one assess whether a theory is well expressed in a computer model?

The first step is obvious and should be done while the model is being designed (although it is a good idea to go back and check after the model is built). Is the basic structure of the model—its variables, parameters, and data types—equivalent to that of the theory? For example, a classic theory of human psychology describes cognition as a set of procedures on two structural components: long-term memory and working memory. A computational model of the theory must represent these two components; otherwise, it is a model of a different theory. Assuming that the basic structural form of the theory is preserved in the model, how can we judge the representation of process?

First, one might use face validity, as described above. Ask experts familiar with the theory if the model's processes capture the theory. Second, the model should be run for special cases in which the processing and outcome in the theory are known. These might be simplified forms of the theory for which mathematical analysis is tractable, in which case the model's outcome and processes, with initial conditions set to match the special case, must match what is known to be true.

For example, Jones, Radcliff, Taber, and Timpone (1995) tested the internal validity of their model of social choice by comparing its output to values computed analytically. They were interested in estimating the probability of achieving a majority winner in an election given varying sizes of electorates, numbers of voting alternatives, and assumptions about the nature of individual preferences. Values for small electorates and few alternatives are well known, given the assumption that voters are never indifferent between pairs of alternatives—that is, closed form solutions have been found under these restrictions. The estimates generated by the model exactly matched these known values, strongly supporting the validity of the model as a representation of social choice theory. The model was then used to estimate the probability of a majority winner under new conditions and new assumptions about individual preferences, for which closed form solutions have not been obtained.

This example raises the further issue of reliability, akin to the empirical concern with consistency in repeated measures. When stochastic uncertainty is incorporated in models, as it is in the social choice example, we must consider consistency over multiple runs. For one thing, the value of estimates from a highly stochastic model depends on how consistent they are, which depends on whether enough runs have been done. Fortunately, this is checked easily in a probabilistic computational model by systematically comparing the multiple runs until they converge on a robust estimate. Jones et al. (1995) ran their model a million times for each set of initial conditions, getting estimates stable to the third decimal. This idea of multiple iterations of the same model can be used no matter how many stochastic components are included in a model. In fact, the control a researcher has over computational models allows explicit tinkering and manipulation of these components to see how each reacts when others are held constant or even when basic processes are altered. For example, one often does not know from a theory whether key stochastic elements are interactive or additive; in a computational model, both forms can be examined.

A third method for judging the internal validity of process mechanisms is sensitivity analysis. When rendering theories as computer programs, specific choices must be made, including parameter values, the ranges of values for the initial conditions, and the sampling methods and probability distributions for stochastic elements. Even adaptive models have initial conditions and parameter values that must comport with the theory or problem being represented. In sensitivity analysis, one systematically varies the values of parameters or other model components (e.g., probability distributions) to see how the model's conclusions are affected. This allows the modeler to distinguish those parameters for which small changes influence model performance from those for which almost any plausible value will produce much the same result. Consider again POLI, the expert system of U.S. policy toward Asia in the 1950s. An important issue was the sensitivity of the model to uncertainty at two levels. First, the theory suggested that the model should be very sensitive to changes in the overall balance of belief systems, or paradigms, in the policy-making community. Second, the model should be sensitive to changes in core beliefs (those with high certainty factors) but not sensitive to changes in peripheral beliefs (low CFs). These factors were varied systematically, and model performance was tracked. Fortunately, POLI performed as expected in the theory (Taber, 1992). Had it not, changes in the model would have been necessary.

Once we are convinced that a model is internally valid, we can use sensitivity analysis to examine the importance of theoretical assumptions. Modeling leads to simplifying assumptions about the real world. It is useful to be able to see what effect various simplifications have. If it turns out that the important qualitative conclusions from a model do not change when a constraint is relaxed, it may be safe to make the assumption; if not, the nature of the assumption may warrant closer attention. Sensitivity analysis serves as a warning mechanism and a guide to model development beyond the initial model representation. Finally, as noted in earlier sections of this chapter, sensitivity analysis can also be used to facilitate both outcome and process validation.

Beauty

Although Beauty truly is in the eye of the beholder, aesthetic criteria cannot be ignored in evaluating a model, computational or otherwise. Lave and March (1993) suggest three attributes that make a model aesthetically pleasing: simplicity (parsimony), fertility, and surprise. These criteria are not simply matters of taste and are worthy of serious consideration by social scientists attempting to represent real-world systems.

Parsimony

In general, modeling seeks a simplified understanding of real-world systems or theories. Models focus on core theoretical components at the expense of complete, presumably superfluous detail. This goes back to William of Occam's view, *"Non sunt multipicanda entia praeter necessitatem,"* which means literally "Things should not be multiplied without good reason" (Starfield, Smith, & Bleloch, 1990, p. 19). The problem with parsimony is the inherent ambiguity over what constitutes a "good reason" for "multiplying things." To some extent, parsimony treads on the domain of accuracy and validity already discussed.

There is no doubt that simplicity is seductive, but is this a fatal attraction? Parsimony generally has been a very useful heuristic for physics, but some biologists consider it misleading (Crick, 1988). The question remains: Where should the social sciences be on Occam's dimension? One danger is that simplicity, which should always be subservient to truth, may become confused with it. A desire for simplicity that drives us to accept obviously invalid models will not lead us to causal understanding. On the other hand, some simulation projects become too complex to be fully understood. If we cannot, after the fact, clearly trace how our artificial world generated its behavior, we are in deep trouble. It is a balancing act: As Occam implied, one should judge a model first by whether it accurately represents the important processes and second by whether it successfully eliminates the unimportant ones. Clearly, parsimony is not purely aesthetic; it must include a utilitarian component.

Fertility and Surprise

Fertility refers to the number and quality of a model's implications and the degree to which it can be generalized. First, there is little dispute that, all else being equal, more predictions are better than few predictions. This is true on both theoretical and empirical grounds, for a model that makes many predictions is a richer framework for theoretical deductions and is far easier to test. Fertility is related to parsimony, because in assessing the fertility of a model, we should control for the number of its assumptions. Highly complex models must generate more implications than simpler ones to be considered fertile. Although we do not always favor simplicity, we do think it reasonable to expect more of complex models. In general, we are suspicious of highly complex models that generate few predictions. On the other hand, we must also consider the quality of a model's implications. A complex model that makes far more "finely grained" predictions is preferable to a simpler one that only paints broad strokes. We also should consider the generalizability of a model's implications. Models and theories that explain a wider range of phenomena should be preferred to narrower ones. Once again, aesthetics has much to do with pragmatics.

An important dimension of fertility is surprise. By surprising us, powerful models generate unexpected predictions that ideally can be tested. An implication may be surprising because we have not thought of it before, though it fits well with what we believe, or because it is counterintuitive, meaning that it does not fit easily with what we believe. In either case, precision and surprise go hand in hand, and even seemingly simple theories can yield surprising implications when modeled explicitly. Very simple theories, however, are less likely to surprise us than are complex ones, because they can be "mentally simulated," yielding their implications without recourse to deduction from formal models. Complex theories of the sort that require computational modeling therefore are more likely to generate surprising conclusions.

The combination of fertility and surprise allows for the greatest contribution to scientific understanding. At worst, when new predictions are found to be inaccurate, models can be refined and improved or discarded (also an advance for science). At best, models that make new and unexpected predictions that do pan out under empirical testing can extend our theoretical understanding. Once again, we have found utilitarian factors in an aesthetic judgment.

Justice

The criterion of Justice is less universally accepted than either Truth or Beauty, though normative concerns clearly influence social science. Beyond agreeing with Lave and March's quaint idealism that we should pursue justice in our models as in our lives, and qualifying that sentiment with a pragmatic warning that our models should serve truth, however distasteful, we have little to say on the subject.

One aspect of Justice as a criterion for assessing computational models does warrant mention. Computational models have a practical role to play in normative research related to the possibility of counterfactual simulation. Verified models of policy-relevant processes can be used to "discover" the implications of a range of policy alternatives. Consider the issue of health care. If a good model of the impact of health care plans on various segments of the population existed, it could be used to examine the merits of public versus private, single-payer versus distributed, or federal versus state-run programs. Particularly relevant from a normative perspective would be the impact of these policies on different socioeconomic classes.

On the other hand, to the extent that models have an influence on policy and debate, accuracy is even more important, lest we run the risk of making

82

things worse. For example, a clerical error in programming the original *Limits to Growth* report of the Club of Rome led directly to many of the most dire predictions about the collapse of civilization (personal communication from Philip Schrodt). The failure to catch this mistake during debugging still has effects on the policy debate over population and pollution.

Conclusion

We all aspire to perfection, but experience brings us back to earth. A perfect model is true, beautiful, and just. In the real world, we make compromises among these ideals. Although these standards are familiar, computational modeling changes somewhat how we apply them. Truth divides into internal validity, outcome validity, and for many computational projects, process validity. Testing internal validity, using the tools of sensitivity analysis, is more involved and systematic than would be necessary for simpler models. Outcome validation follows the conventional logic of quantitative social science, but there are new problems, most notably related to degrees of freedom. Process validation has not been a goal of most quantitative social scientists, so many of the issues are unfamiliar. We suggest variations on face validation, direct testing of assumptions (especially those shown to be important during sensitivity analysis), and multilevel testing.

The most important standard of Beauty traditionally has been parsimony. Simplicity is still a goal in computational models, but when the essential processes to be represented are complex, truth requires the model to be complex. Fertility and surprise remain important goals for computational modeling. Indeed, computational models are more likely to yield surprising implications than are simpler models. Although Justice certainly has a role in social sciences, we emphasize the greater importance of truth.

Such a description of evaluation criteria illustrates the realization that modelers, computational or otherwise, are as much artisans as scientists, and to the uninitiated they may look like "witch doctors" (Schrodt, 1991a). Our hope is that this monograph will dispel some of this mystery, revealing the tools of computational modeling to be useful and practical additions to the repertoire of social science methods.

APPENDIX: GLOSSARY OF TERMS

Antecedent: The IF part of an IF-THEN production rule; also called the condition.

Artificial intelligence (AI):   A broad modeling approach forged from the intersection of computer science, engineering, philosophy, cognitive science, and psychology.

Backward chaining: A control method for inference chaining that fires a rule when its consequent is believed to be true; used to discover the conditions that would allow some final goal to be achieved.

Bit strings: Information represented as a sequence of binary digits (e.g., 011001).

Case-based reasoning: A modeling approach in which knowledge is represented by reference to past experiences, which are stored in memory as cases; inferences about new situations are generated by looking at what has happened in similar cases in the past.

Cellular automata: A type of dynamic simulation that models discrete dynamic systems of interacting units, where the units are very simple and the rules of interaction local; interaction is limited to the immediate neighborhood of a cell.

Certainty factor (CF):   A numerical index of the degree of belief in a piece of information; assumes values from -1 to 1.

Chromosomes: The "genetic material" of a genetic algorithm model; store current solutions to the problem.

Connectionism (parallel distributed processing, or PDP):   An AI approach that represents knowledge as states of activation distributed throughout a large neural network; part of their appeal is based on an analogy to brain structure, leading some to argue that they represent more fundamental processes than do other AI methods.

Consequent: The THEN part of an IF-THEN production rule; also called the action.

Control: The part of an inference mechanism that determines the order in which inferences are made and which of several competing inferences are made.

Counterfactual analysis: The examination of events that did not actually happen using a model of the system; for example, one might use a model of U.S. presidential decision making to ask what U.S. policy toward Vietnam would have been had John F. Kennedy survived.

Declarative knowledge: The part of knowledge that defines concepts and their relations; for example, knowledge of chess is partly an understanding of the names of the pieces and the arrangement of the board; compare with procedural knowledge.

Default reasoning: An inference mechanism, closely related to inheritance, that allows reasoning from incomplete information in a semantic network or frame system; for example, we might infer that Tweety the bird can fly even though we have never seen Tweety fly, because that is the default for birds.

Delta rule: A learning rule for neural networks that adapts connection weights incrementally until the desired output is achieved.

Dynamic simulation: One of the oldest approaches to simulation, used to model process flow with mathematically expressed state equations that define system dynamics; usually the histories of these models through time are analyzed.

Entropy: A measure of the uncertainty remaining in the classification of objects, as in ID3; the greater the reduction in entropy achieved by a classification system, the greater the gain in information.

Evaluation function: For genetic algorithm models, the function for deciding survivability; evaluates the quality of a solution to the problem.

Expert systems: Knowledge-based models that usually rely on a rule base to represent human expertise; they are by far the most widely used AI modeling technique, finding many practical applications in business and government as well as for research.

Face validity: The subjective assessment of a model's validity, based on general knowledge of the research domain; sometimes panels of experts are consulted; see internal validity.

Forward chaining: A control method for inference chaining that fires a rule when its antecedent is believed to be true; used to infer the implications of initial conditions.

Frame: One of the "large, complex chunks" of knowledge from a frame system, representing knowledge about a particular concept.

Frame systems: A knowledge representation method that assumes that knowledge is organized in large, complex chunks, which are linked associatively.

Genetic algorithms: (1) a class of computational model that simulates evolutionary processes using insights from population dynamics; (2) the rules used for constructing the chromosomes of offspring from those of their parents, including mutation, inversion, and crossover.

Hybrid systems: Computational models that use more than one representation formalism.

ID3: An inductive learning algorithm for extracting classification rules from a set of examples, usually in the form of a simple rectangular data file in which each example is a case and each variable is a qualitative feature.

Inference chaining: The principal inference mechanism for rule-based systems, it adds the consequent of a rule to working memory when the antecedent is believed to be true; chains may grow when newly inferred information allows more rules to fire.

Inference engine (rule interpreter): The part of an expert system that contains its inference mechanisms; it applies prior knowledge from the knowledge base to new information to generate new inferences.

Inheritance: An inference mechanism in which objects in a hierarchical semantic network or frame system acquire the attributes of classes to which they belong.

Initial population: The starting set of solutions to the problem in a genetic algorithm model, stored as chromosomes.

Initial values or conditions: The starting values of parameters and variables in a dynamic simulation.

Internal validity: The degree of correspondence between a model and the theory it represents; see face validity.

Knowledge base: The part of an expert system that stores the system's prior beliefs and knowledge, in the form of rules or frames; sometimes called the rule base.

Knowledge engineering: The process of extracting the knowledge of human experts through interviews, observations, or archival research.

Knowledge representation hypothesis: All intelligent processing is based on stored information, organized in such a way that it can be applied to the processing of new information.

Layered feedforward systems: A type of neural network in which propagation of activation passes through the network in a forward direction through three types of layers of units: An input layer, one or more hidden layers, and an output layer.

Matching: An inference mechanism for frame systems and rule-based systems that compares expressions to see if they are similar enough to be considered equivalent; similarity must be defined strictly.

Monte Carlo methods: Methods for exploring variations in random numbers within a simulation.

Neural networks: The representation language for connectionism, based on a loose analogy with the brain; simple processing units (neurons) are densely linked to other processing units; knowledge arises from the overall configuration of links and activation throughout the network.

Numerical analysis: Computing the output from a model for a wide range of numerical inputs; used to discover the behavior of a formal model through brute force when more elegant analytic solutions are difficult or impossible to apply.

Outcome validity: The degree of correspondence between a model's predictions and real-world data; contrast with process validity.

Parallel processing: Procedures are carried out simultaneously, so that order makes no difference; for a modeling approach, see connectionism.

Phenomenal system: The real-world system a model represents.

Postdiction: As opposed to prediction, this means that the outputs of a model are meant to correspond with events that have already happened.

Primitive structure of a knowledge representation: The most basic structure of a knowledge representation language, defining its syntax, inference mechanisms, and semantics; syntax concerns the formal notation, inference mechanisms define the permissible processes on information, and semantics concern the meanings of the knowledge stored.

Procedural knowledge: The part of knowledge that defines how to do things; for example, knowledge of chess is partly the set of actions one can take; compare with declarative knowledge.

Process validity: The degree of correspondence between a model's mechanisms and real-world processes; contrast with outcome validity.

Production rules: Representations for conditional knowledge, using the form IF {condition} THEN {action}.

Propagation: For neural networks, this refers to the process of spreading activation; it computes the net input to a unit as the sum of activation from all connected units multiplied by the connection weights.

Prototyping: The process of translating an expert's knowledge into the formal representation of a knowledge base in an expert system; the process leads to the gradual improvement of the expert system as it iterates through prototype-test cycles.

Reliability: The level of robustness of stochastic models.

Rule-based systems: Knowledge is represented as a set of domain-specific propositions in IF-THEN form.

Semantic network: A knowledge representation method that uses a node-link metaphor to display the relationships among concepts in memory; most commonly used by cognitive scientists who have an associative view of human memory.

Sensitivity analysis: A set of procedures to illuminate the inner workings of a complex model and to discover which parts of a model are responsible for a particular output; also used to check model validity and reliability.

Serial processing: Procedures are carried out in sequence, one after another, so that order of processing makes a difference.

Slots: The entries that define properties in a frame; slot names define the type of property; slot fillers define the value of the property; for example, a frame for a political candidate might have a slot named "party ID" with a filler "Republican."

Spreading activation: An inferencing mechanism for semantic networks in which attention is spread across links from node to node.

State equations: The set of mathematical equations that define behavior in a dynamic system model, where behavior means changes in the state of the model.

State variables: The set of variables whose values at a given time fully define the current state of a dynamic system model.

Token node: A node in a semantic network linked to a type node; representing a component of the meaning of a type node, as "young" and "person" are parts of the definition of "child."

Turing test: A test of validity; if a model's output and/or processes are indistinguishable from the real system's output and/or processes, it is valid; the original version only concerned output comparisons, though the idea has been extended to include process validation; Turing (1950) suggested this principle as a practical way of deciding whether computer programs could exhibit intelligence.

Type node: A node in a semantic network representing a concept; the meaning of the concept is broken into components (token nodes); for example, "child" might be defined as a "young" "person."

Working memory: The part of an expert system in which currently believed facts and new inferences are stored; a scratchpad for inferences.

REFERENCES

ABELSON, R. P., and CARROLL, J. D. (1965) "Computer simulation of individual belief systems." *American Behavioral Scientist, 8,* 24-30.

ADELI, H., and HUNG, S. (1995) *Machine Learning: Neural Networks, Genetic Algorithms, and Fuzzy Systems.* New York: Wiley.

ANDERSON, J. R. (1983) *The Architecture of Cognition.* Cambridge, MA: Harvard University Press.

AXELROD, R. (Ed.). (1976) *Structure of Decision: The Cognitive Maps of Political Elite.* Princeton, NJ: Princeton University Press.

AXELROD, R. (1984) *The Evolution of Cooperation.* New York: Basic Books.

AXELROD, R. (1987) "The evolution of strategies in the iterated prisoner's dilemma." In L. Davis (Ed.), *Genetic Algorithms and Simulated Annealing.* London: Pitman.

BARR, A., and FEIGENBAUM, E. A. (Eds.). (1981) *The Handbook of Artificial Intelligence, Vol. I.* Reading, MA: Addison-Wesley.

BENDOR, J., and MOE, T. M. (1985) "An adaptive model of bureaucratic politics." *American Political Science Review, 79,* 755-774.

BENFER, R. A., BRENT, E. E., and FURBEE, L. (1991) *Expert Systems.* Sage University Paper series on Quantitative Applications in the Social Sciences, 07-077. Newbury Park, CA: Sage.

BLUM, A. (1992) *Neural Networks in C++: An Object-Oriented Framework for Building Connectionist Systems.* New York: Wiley.

BOLLEN, K. A. (1989) *Structural Equations With Latent Variables.* New York: Wiley.

BOYNTON, G. R., and LODGE, M. (1994) "Voter's image of candidates." In A. H. Miller and B. E. Gronbeck (Eds.), *Presidential Campaigns and American Self Images.* Boulder, CO: Westview.

BREMER, S. A., and MIHALKA, M. (1977) "Machiavelli in machina: Or politics among hexagons." In K. W. Deutsch (Ed.), *Problems of World Modeling.* Boston: Ballinger.

BRODBECK, M. (1969) "Models, meaning, and theories." In L. Gross (Ed.), *Symposium on Sociological Theory.* New York: Harper.

CARRICO, M. A., GIRARD, J. E., and JONES, J. P. (1989) *Building Knowledge Systems: Developing and Managing Rule-Based Applications.* New York: McGraw-Hill.

COHEN, P. R., and FEIGENBAUM, E. A. (Eds.). (1982) *The Handbook of Artificial Intelligence, Vol. III.* Reading, MA: Addison-Wesley.

COWEN, R. A., and MILLER, J. H. (1990) *Economic Life on a Lattice* (Santa Fe Institute Working Paper 90-010). Santa Fe, NM: Santa Fe Institute.

CRICK, F. (1988) *What Mad Pursuit: A Personal View of Scientific Discovery.* New York: Basic Books.

CUSACK, T. R., and STOLL, R. J. (1990) *Exploring Realpolitik: Probing International Relations Theory With Computer Simulation.* Boulder, CO: Lynne Rienner.

89

90

DAVIS, L., and STEENSTRUP, M. (1987) "Genetic algorithms and simulated annealing: An overview." In L. Davis (Ed.), *Genetic Algorithms and Simulated Annealing.* London: Pitman.

DUFFY, G., and TUCKER, S. A. (1995) "Political science: Artificial intelligence applications." *Social Science Computer Review, 13,* 1-20.

EYSENCK, M. W., and KEANE, M. T. (1990) *Cognitive Psychology: A Student's Handbook.* Hillsdale, NJ: Lawrence Erlbaum.

FARMER, D., TOFFOLI, T., and WOLFRAM, S. (Eds.). (1984) *Cellular Automata.* New York: North-Holland.

FINDLER, N. V. (Ed.). (1979) *Associative Networks: Representation and Use of Knowledge by Computers.* New York: Academic Press.

FIORINA, P. (1975) "Formal Models in Political Science." *American Journal of Political Science, 19,* 133-159.

FORRESTER, J. W. (1969) *Urban Dynamics.* Cambridge, MA: MIT Press.

FURBEE, L. (1989) "A folk expert system: Soils classification in the Colca Valley, Peru." *Anthropological Quarterly, 62,* 83-102.

GARSON, G. D. (1990) "Expert systems: An overview for social scientists." *Social Science Computer Review, 8,* 387-410.

GARSON, G. D. (1991) "A comparison of neural network and expert systems algorithms with common multivariate procedures for analysis of social science data." *Social Science Computer Review, 9,* 399-434.

GARSON, G. D. (1994) "Social science computer simulation: Its history, design, and future." *Social Science Computer Review, 12,* 55-82.

GEORGE, A. L. (1969) "The operational code: A neglected approach to the study of political leaders and decision-making." *International Studies Quarterly, 13,* 190-222.

GEORGE, A. L., and SMOKE, R. (1974) *Deterrence in American Foreign Policy: Theory and Practice.* New York: Columbia University Press.

GOLDBERG, D. E. (1989) *Genetic Algorithms in Search, Optimization, and Machine Learning.* Reading, MA: Addison-Wesley.

GRZYMALA-BUSSE, J. W. (1991) *Managing Uncertainty in Expert Systems.* Boston: Kluwer Academic.

GUILLET, D. (Ed.). (1989) "Expert-systems applications in anthropology." *Anthropological Quarterly, 62,* 57-102.

GUTOWITZ, H. (Ed.). (1991) *Cellular Automata: Theory and Experiment.* Cambridge, MA: MIT Press.

HAKEN, H. (1983) *Advanced Synergetics.* Berlin: Springer-Verlag.

HANNON, B., and RUTH, M. (1994) *Dynamic Modeling.* New York: Springer-Verlag.

HASTIE, R. (1988) "A computer simulation model of person memory." *Journal of Experimental Social Psychology, 24,* 423-447.

HOLLAND, J. H. (1975) *Adaptation in Natural and Artificial Systems.* Ann Arbor: University of Michigan Press.

HOOVER, S. V., and PERRY, R. F. (1990) *Simulation: A Problem-Solving Approach.* Reading, MA: Addison-Wesley.

HUCKFELDT, R. R., KOHFELD, C. W., and LIKENS, T. W. (1982) *Dynamic Modeling: An Introduction.* Sage University Paper series on Quantitative Applications in the Social Sciences, 07-027. Newbury Park, CA: Sage.

HUNT, E. B., MARIN, J., and STONE, P. J. (1966) *Experiments in Induction.* New York: Academic Press.

JONES, B., RADCLIFF, B., TABER, C., and TIMPONE, R. (1995) "Condorcet winners and the paradox of voting: Probability calculations for weak preference orders." *American Political Science Review, 89,* 137-144.

KAHNEMAN, D., and TVERSKY, A. (1979) "Prospect theory: An analysis of decision under risk." *Econometrica, 47,* 263-291.

KANDEL, A. (Ed.). (1992) *Fuzzy Expert Systems.* Boca Raton, FL: CRC.

KHANNA, T. (1990) *Foundations of Neural Networks.* Reading, MA: Addison-Wesley.

KHEIR, N. A. (Ed.). (1988) *Systems Modeling and Computer Simulation.* New York: Marcel Dekker.

KING, G., KEOHANE, R. O., and VERBA, S. (1994) *Designing Social Inquiry: Scientific Inference in Qualitative Research.* Princeton, NJ: Princeton University Press.

KODRATOFF, Y., and MICHALSKI, R. S. (Eds.). (1990) *Machine Learning: An Artificial Intelligence Approach, Vol. III.* San Mateo, CA: Morgan Kaufmann.

KOESTLER, A. (1959) *The Sleepwalkers.* New York: Universal.

KOLODNER, J. L. (1992) "An introduction to case-based reasoning." *Artificial Intelligence Review, 6,* 3-34.

KOLODNER, J. L. (1993) *Case-Based Reasoning.* San Francisco: Morgan Kaufmann.

LAVE, C. A., and MARCH, J. G. (1993) *An Introduction to Models in the Social Sciences.* New York: University Press of America.

McNEILL, F. M., and THRO, E. (1994) *Fuzzy Logic: A Practical Approach.* Boston: AP Professional.

McPHEE, W. N. (1963) *Formal Theories of Mass Behavior.* New York: Free Press.

MEADOWS, D. H., MEADOWS, D. L., RANDERS, J., and BEHRENS, W. W. (1972) *The Limits to Growth.* New York: Universe Books.

MICHALSKI, R. S., CARBONELL, J. G., and MITCHELL, T. M. (Eds.). (1983) *Machine Learning: An Artificial Intelligence Approach, Vol. I.* Los Altos, CA: Morgan Kaufmann.

MICHALSKI, R. S., CARBONELL, J. G., and MITCHELL, T. M. (Eds.) (1986) *Machine Learning: An Artificial Intelligence Approach, Vol. II.* Los Altos, CA: Morgan Kaufmann.

MICHALSKI, R. S., and TECUCI, G. (Eds.). (1994) *Machine Learning: A Multistrategy Approach, Vol. IV.* San Francisco: Morgan Kaufmann.

MINSKY, M. (1975) "A framework for representing knowledge." In P. Winston (Ed.), *The Psychology of Computer Vision.* New York: McGraw-Hill.

NISKANEN, W. (1975) "Bureaucrats and politicians." *Journal of Law and Economics, 18,* 617-644.

OSTROM, T. M. (1988) "Computer simulation: The third symbol system." *Journal of Experimental Social Psychology, 24,* 381-392.

PEDERSEN, K. (1989) *Expert Systems Programming: Practical Techniques for Rule-Based Systems.* New York: Wiley.

PELTZMAN, S. (1976) "Toward a more general theory of regulation." *Journal of Law and Economics, 19,* 211-240.

QUILLIAN, R. (1968) "Semantic memory." In M. Minsky (Ed.), *Semantic Information Processing.* Cambridge, MA: MIT Press.

QUINLAN, J. R. (1979) "Discovering rules by induction from large collections of examples." In D. Michie (Ed.), *Expert Systems in the Micro Electronic Age.* Edinburgh, UK: Edinburgh University Press.

QUINLAN, J. R. (1986) "Induction of decision trees." *Machine Learning, 1,* 81-106.

92

RAWLINS, G. J. E. (Ed.). (1991) *Foundations of Genetic Algorithms.* San Mateo, CA: Morgan Kaufmann.

REICHGELT, H. (1991) *Knowledge Representation: An AI Perspective.* Norwood, NJ: Ablex.

RIETMAN, E. (1989) *Exploring the Geometry of Nature: Computer Modeling of Chaos, Fractals, Cellular Automata, and Neural Networks.* Blue Ridge Summit, PA: Windcrest.

RISSLAND, E., and ASHLEY, K. (1987) "HYPO: A case-based reasoning system." Proceedings of IJCAI-87, Milan, Italy.

RUMELHART, D. E., and McCLELLAND, J. L. (Eds.). (1989) *Explorations in Parallel Distributed Processing.* Cambridge, MA: MIT Press.

SCHALKOFF, R. (1992) *Pattern Recognition: Statistical, Structural, and Neural Approaches.* New York: Wiley.

SCHANK, R., and ABELSON, R. (1977) *Scripts, Plans, Goals, and Understandings: An Inquiry into Human Knowledge Structures.* Hillsdale, NJ: Lawrence Erlbaum.

SCHRODT, P. A. (1991a) "Political methodology explained." *Political Methodologist,* 4(2), 19.

SCHRODT, P. A. (1991b) "Prediction of interstate conflict outcomes using a neural network." *Social Science Computer Review, 9,* 359-380.

SCHRODT, P. A. (in press) *Patterns, Rules and Learning: Computational Models of International Behavior.* Ann Arbor: University of Michigan Press.

SLADE, S. (1994) *Goal-Based Decision Making: An Interpersonal Model.* Hillsdale, NJ: Lawrence Erlbaum.

SNYDER, R. C., BRUCK, H. W., and SAPIN, B. (1962) *Foreign Policy Decision Making: An Approach to the Study of International Politics.* New York: Free Press.

STARFIELD, A. M., SMITH, K. A., and BLELOCH, A. L. (1990) *How to Model It: Problem Solving for the Computer Age.* New York: McGraw-Hill.

SYLVAN, D. A., GOEL, A., and CHANDRASEKARAN, B. (1990) "Analyzing political decision making from an information processing perspective: JESSE." *American Journal of Political Science, 34,* 74-123.

TABER, C. S. (1991) *The Policy Arguer: A Computational Model of U.S. Foreign Policy Belief Systems in the 1950s.* Ph.D. dissertation, University of Illinois at Urbana-Champaign.

TABER, C. S. (1992) "POLI: An expert system model of U.S. foreign policy belief systems." *American Political Science Review, 86,* 888-904.

TABER, C. S. (1993) "National arms acquisition as a rational competitive process." *Simulation and Gaming, 24,* 413-428.

TABER, C. S., and STEENBERGEN, M. (1995) "Computational experiments in electoral behavior." In M. Lodge and K. McGraw (Eds.), *Political Information Processing.* Ann Arbor: University of Michigan Press.

TABER, C. S., and TIMPONE, R. (1994a) "Pictures in the PC: Computational modeling and political psychology." In M. X. Delli-Carpini, L. Huddy, and R. Y. Shapiro (Eds.), *New Directions in Political Psychology.* Greenwich, CT: JAI.

TABER, C. S., and TIMPONE, R. (1994b) "The Policy Arguer: The architecture of an expert system." *Social Science Computer Review, 12,* 1-25.

THOMPSON, B., and THOMPSON, W. (1986) "Finding rules in data." *Byte, 11*(12), 149-158.

TURING, A. M. (1950) "Computing machinery and intelligence." *Mind, 59,* 433-460.

UNSELD, S. D., and MALLERY, J. C. (1993) *Interaction Detection in Complex Datamodels* (A. I. Memo No. 1298). Cambridge, MA: MIT Artificial Intelligence Laboratory.

WEBER, R. P. (1990) *Basic Content Analysis, 2nd Edition.* Sage University Paper series on Quantitative Applications in the Social Sciences, 07-049. Newbury Park, CA: Sage.

WHICKER, M. L., and SIGELMAN, L. (1991) *Computer Simulation Applications: An Introduction* (Applied Social Research Methods Series, Vol. 25). Newbury Park, CA: Sage.

WINSTON, P. H. (1984) *Artificial Intelligence* (2nd ed.). Reading, MA: Addison-Wesley.

YOUNG, M. D. (1994) *Foreign Policy Problem Representation and President Carter.* Ph.D. dissertation, The Ohio State University, Columbus, OH.

ZADEH, L., and KACPRZYK, J. (Eds.). (1992) *Fuzzy Logic for the Management of Uncertainty.* New York: John Wiley and Sons.

ABOUT THE AUTHORS

CHARLES S. TABER is Assistant Professor of Political Science at the State University of New York at Stony Brook, where he teaches political psychology, international relations, and computational modeling. He received his Ph.D. from the University of Illinois at Urbana-Champaign, where he worked at the Merriam Laboratory for Analytic Political Research. He currently is working on formal models of political cognition, with applications to the evaluation of political candidates and the decision making of foreign policy elites.

RICHARD J. TIMPONE is Assistant Professor of Political Science at the State University of New York at Stony Brook, where he teaches American government and statistical analysis. He received his Ph.D. from the State University of New York at Stony Brook. His current research interests focus on the relationship between institutional factors and individual behavior, with an emphasis on electoral behavior.